Daily Life

in

The Republic of Texas

By Joseph William Schmitz, S. M.

Copano Bay Press
2007

Originally published in 1935 under the title
Thus They Lived: Social Life in the Republic of Texas

Copano Bay Press Edition

ISBN: 978-0-9767799-3-3

Library of Congress Control Number: 2007925646

TABLE OF CONTENTS

Preface

This little sketch aims to tell the story of the daily life of the early Texans. In matter of time it covers the period of the Republic, 1836–1845. There are already many books in print that record the events of the Republic and that glorify its outstanding heroes. All the principal happenings, the civil and military accomplishments of the leaders of the nation, and the sensational work of some of the better known of the forefathers have been written. But the story of the ordinary activities of the people who inhabited the Republic has usually been neglected by the general writers. It is this story that is to be told here.

The activities and accomplishments of the pioneers, their daily struggle for existence, their problems and how they solved them, their distractions and amusements — in short their daily life — when once understood and properly appreciated command respect and esteem. This book is written with the hope that it will instill a respect for the efforts, an appreciation for the achievements and a deep admiration for the accomplishments of those sturdy pioneers who first lived in this land.

In preparing this study I have drawn largely from the letters, diaries, and writings of the early inhabitants themselves; I have taken much from the writings of the visitors to the country, and in particular from the writings of the Englishman William E. Bollaert who resided and traveled in Texas during the years 1840–1844, and whose voluminous manuscript, hitherto practically unused, is in the Newberry Library, Chicago, Illinois. Most of the other manuscript material is located in the archives of the University of Texas, Austin. I have quoted much, sometimes at length. I have done so in order to preserve the spirit of the original, to give the picture completely and accurately, and, as it were, to let the pioneers themselves tell the story; it is most exact that way.

I wish to acknowledge my gratitude to Miss Allie Welsh of the San Antonio Public Library for valuable assistance in locating material for this paper. I am also indebted to Mrs. Mattie Austin Hatcher, archivist of the University of Texas for courtesies shown me while working with material under her charge. My sincere thanks are likewise due to Dr. Paul Kiniery of Loyola University, Chicago, Illinois, for valuable suggestions and critical assistance.

JOSEPH W. SCHMITZ, S. M.
St. Marys University,
San Antonio, Texas.

"Desperate Whittlers of Sticks..."
The People of Texas

This account of the social conditions in Texas during the period of the Republic will be limited to the activities of the Anglo-Americans since they constituted the overwhelming majority of the inhabitants. True, there were many other nationalities represented, notably the Mexicans and Germans. But the Mexicans were practically limited to San Antonio and the extreme west, with small settlements in the old towns of Nacogdoches and Goliad. The more progressive and industrious Mexicans refused to live under the Anglo-Americans, and went back to their native land when Texas became a republic. Those who remained were a class unto themselves; their customs, dress, manners, and culture were essentially the same as those of their forefathers. They still enjoyed their daily siesta, still used the family *metate* for grinding Indian corn into pulp to prepare it for baking their tortilla bread. These people were not assimilated, but neither did they in the least retard the progressive Americans.

The Germans also came to Texas in considerable numbers, particularly in the last years of the Republic. Those who came in these declining years preserved their national traits. Those who came earlier readily mingled, under the primitive conditions of the frontier, with their English-speaking neighbors so that their lives and habits were soon similar to those of the Anglo-Americans. The same may safely be said of the other nationalities.

Excepting, therefore, the Mexicans and Germans, most of the inhabitants of Texas were immigrants from the slave-holding states of the Union. These came for a variety of reasons: some merely loved an adventurous life, others desired to escape the restraints of the more settled communities, but the vast majority sought to profit by the opportunities offered in the new land. Such people were generally men and women of initiative, energy, and ambition, traits which were all accentuated by the hardships and rewards of pioneer life. Quarrelsome, rude, boastful, vulgar, they were as someone has fittingly said, "men with the bark on."

The majority of the inhabitants migrating from the frontier states were substantially of the same type as those that stayed and built up their own regions. It has been stated that "from the commencement of Austin's Colony the settlers were generally people of good character; and since the revolution, the United States have not only lost much population and capital, but also much talent and integrity by emigration to Texas."[1] The pioneers came to build their homes in the new land, to provide for their future and the future of their children. With this outlook on life there was usually a public opinion sufficiently strong to keep the standard of conduct on a fairly high plane.

The writings of visitors and early settlers are replete with favorable reflections on the inhabitants. An Englishman reported that he had "found as much good judgment, real worth & intelligence in Texas, as I ever met with in the U. S." and in "accomplishment & intellect...[they will] vie or bear comparison with the proudest & best of your land."[2] Another writer records that despite their deficiency in book knowledge, they were "...abundantly capable in dealing with the perplexities of pioneer life...they were versatile, self-reliant and sturdy."[3] Often they are classified as being similar in morals, habits, customs, language, and manners, to the citizens of the United States.[4] Lubbock, an early settler who later became influential in politics and finally governor of the State, remembers them as being "intelligent men...Men and women of good breeding," with society "on

---

1 Arthur Ikin, *Texas*, (London, 1841), 75.

2 The Bryan-Hayes Correspondence in the *Quarterly of the Texas State Historical Association*, XXV, 104. This magazine is published by the Association in Austin, Texas. The first annual volume appeared in 1898. With volume 16 the Association enlarged the scope of the magazine and changed the name to *The Southwestern Historical Quarterly*. Hereafter this work will be cited as *Quarterly*.

3 Rex W. Strickland, History of Fannin County 1836-1843 *Quarterly*, XXXIII, 61.

4 Francis Moore, *Map and Description of Texas*, (Philadelphia, 1840), 26, 27.

a firm, fixed, and honest basis."[5] Major George Erath, who took up residence in the country while it was still under the control of Mexico, was sure that the early settlers of Texas "were honest and cordial and neighborly."[6] The Reverend O. M. Addison, Methodist minister of note during the Republic, traveled about a great deal in the Montgomery Circuit, and had a chance to observe the people from a minister's point of view. He speaks most favorably of them:

> In this particular region and extending westward, the people were singularly free from that lawlessness, dishonesty and turbulence, so long supposed by those at a distance to dominate the country. Indeed, their politeness and general good behavior, was a matter of agreeable surprise, and frequent remark, on the part of visitors and newcomers.[7]

It is not to be supposed, however, that all the early Texans were of that sturdy stock. As in all new countries, there were notorious characters who sought refuge there, but never in sufficient numbers to change the general character of society. An unofficial census of one of the early towns divides the population into a resident and a floating one. "The floaters were mostly gamblers…rough, uncivil, fond of fun, whiskey and cards."[8] George Smyth associated with the people while traveling about the Republic surveying land and he is much of the same opinion: "As to the general society of Texas it is as in other new countries, with the superaddition of this circumstance, that being beyond the jurisdiction of the U. S., it has served as a more convenient sanctuary for those who have fled from the pursuit of the laws."[9] An early newspaper editorially calls these men loafers, and reports that the

---

5 Francis Lubbock, *Six Decades in Texas*, (Austin, 1900), 57.

6 Lucy A. Erath, Memoirs of Major George Bernard Erath, *Quarterly*, XXVI, 223.

7 MS. O. M. Addison Papers, April 18, 1834, Dec. 31, 1850, University of Texas, Austin.

8 Janie Lockhard Wallis, *Sixty Years on the Brazos*, (Los Angeles, 1930), 41.

9 Letter undated and unsigned [about 1836], MS. George W. Smyth

community is temporarily rid of them, adding that if they do not return "we shall be willing to rank this beautiful place among the most moral and thriving towns of the republic."[10] Ashbel Smith, an outstanding citizen throughout the period of the Republic and for many years thereafter, in writing his early impressions to his brother, thinks that society is composed "of every degree of morality."[11] A few months later, when he was preparing to leave on a short visit to the United States, he gave strict orders that his office be kept locked at all times: "The City of Houston abounds in thieves," he explained.[12] Mrs. Sam Maverick, probably the first American woman to take up permanent residence in San Antonio, thought that the thieves and wretches who inhabited San Antonio were a serious drawback to the development of that city.[13]

The unwholesome influence of thieves and ruffians upon the general character was fortunately counterbalanced since there was a large percentage of men who were of a distinctly superior type. Among the latter should be counted the government officials and professional men. Then too, there were unusual men who undoubtedly added culture to the pioneer class. A Houston paper as early as 1837 tells us in the following advertisement of an artist in the community: "Jefferson Wright, Portrait Painter, tenders his professional services to the Ladies and Gentlemen of Houston. His gallery of National Portraits will be open to visitors every day at 4."[14] Mr. William E. Bollaert, an English visitor to Texas in the early forties, recalls a pleasant evening spent in Matagorda at the home of Dr. Hunter, a gentleman of culture

---

10 *Telegraph and Texas Register*, (Columbia) Aug 9, 1836 - April 11 1838; (Houston) May 2, 1837-1845; June 23, 1841.

11 Ashbel Smith to George Smith, Houston, Aug. 17 1837 MS Ashbel Smith Papers, 1823-1886, University of Texas, Austin.

12 Smith to Copes, Jan. 7. 1838, MS. Ashbel Smith Papers.

13 Mary A. Maverick to Mrs. A. S. Adams, Sept. 8, 1839 MS Maverick Papers, 1838-1859, University of Texas, Austin. Papers, 1832-1865, Texas State Library, Austin.

14 *Telegraph and Texas Register*, Oct. 11, 1837.

and refinement who was also an accomplished musician: "Violinist as well as Harpist — but above all I subsequently found him a kind friend and good man and excellent companion. The Society I met at his house both of Ladies and Gentlemen left nothing to be desired— beauty, talent and friendship. The 'Belles of Bonasista' were there — they are Mild and fair, gentle as the Zephyr's sigh!"[15]

Certain unsympathetic foreign visitors, however, such as the Englishman Maillard, reported Texas as being a "country filled with habitual liars, drunkards, blasphemers, and slanderers; sanguinary gamesters and cold-blooded assassins; with idleness and sluggish indolence (two vices for which the Texans are already proverbial) with pride, engendered by ignorance & supported by fraud."[16] Furthermore, "en masse they exhibit the features of a ruffianized European mob—to whom however they are inferior in social refinement."[17] These reporters saw only the exceptional and repulsive phases of frontier life; they missed entirely the essential soundness and strength of the pioneer characters that predominated.

Most of the people who came to Texas, as remarked above, had immigrated to take advantage of the opportunities which that land offered them. The correspondence of Stephen F. Austin and Mirabeau B. Lamar contains many letters from people in the United States desiring information about Texas; they wanted to make sure that the land of their adoption would allow them to make a living. Professional men inquired about the chances of bettering their fortunes, speculators asked about fantastic schemes, but the majority wrote to find out about the prospects of making a living on the soil.

---

15 William E. Bollaert, Manuscript, 1840-1844 (2 vols.). I, 88, Newberry Library, Chicago. Bollaert traveled through Texas during the greater part of the time from 1840 to 1844, and took extensive notes with the idea of writing a book about the people. He never wrote the book, and the original manuscript is now in the Newberry library.

16 N. Doran Maillard, *History of the Republic of Texas from the Discovery of the Country to the Present Time*, (London, 1842), 206.

17 Ibid., 212.

After these men were assured of the great opportunities that awaited them, they lost no time in actually immigrating. Visitors to Texas often marveled at the inducements to prospective settlers. Bollaert was particularly impressed by the alluring offers, and wrote in his journal:

> Great bargains in land may be had all over the republic. A large land owner offered to give a friend of mine 2 or 300 acres of good land & build him a house if he would remain in the donor's Neighborhood.
>
> Near San Antonio 1000 acres of fine land were sold for 120 dollars. 500 acres for a pretty good horse etc.
>
> The following bargain was attained a week or two since in Montgomery County. 800 acres with good farm house, out houses, stables all enclosed— 400 head of stock 600 bu. of corn & 200 pigs. Titles for a league of land to be located and 500 acres of located land. All this was offered for 800 dollars cash.[18]

Land was obtained so easily that settlers sometimes had the mistaken idea that it was theirs simply for the taking. Unoccupied lands seemed inviting: Henry Baze must have been annoyed frequently because he inserted a notice in the Columbia newspaper: "This is to forewarn all persons against settling on my league of land on Matagorda Bay, known as the 'half moon point' league."[19] However, it was the ease with which land was obtainable that attracted the agricultural immigrant, and that prompted a Nacogdoches resident to write to his father in Alabama: "There is no country in the world where a living can be procured more easily than in Texas."[20]

---

18 Bollaert, Manuscript, II, 145.
19 *Telegraph and Texas Register*, April -4, 1837.
20 George Smyth to Andrew Smyth, April 14, 1838, MS. George W. Smyth Papers.

Texas did not appeal only to the agricultural class. Many early settlements were anxious to develop into thriving communities and were therefore willing to offer special inducements in the form of donations of land to "Merchants, Artizans, Mechanics & enterprizing people who might choose to settle" in their community in preference to others.[21] Offers of this kind, of course, were not general; but any one who was industrious, whether he was agriculturally inclined or not, found his services in demand.[22] A Houston paper, commenting editorially on the state of affairs in the Republic in 1838, recorded that, excluding the small sections along the western frontier, where conditions were still primitive, all the sections were rejoicing in the general prosperity.[23]

It is impossible to give any authentic figures on the number of people who came to take advantage of these opportunities; it is likewise quite impossible to arrive at a satisfactory estimate of the total population of Texas during the period. Estimates vary from thirty and forty thousand[24] to over two hundred thousand[25], excluding Indians and slaves. But it is certain that most of the immigrants came from the United States, and that they came despite Indian troubles, threats of war with Mexico, and the generally unsettled state of affairs. In 1838 the *Telegraph and Texas Register* carried this news item concerning immigration: "A gentleman who lately arrived from Bastrop, states that immense numbers of emigrants are constantly arriving in that section. He believes that three quarters of the present settlers of that county have arrived since August last."[26] At about the same time another newspaper reported:

---

21 Bollaert. Manuscript, II, 70.

22 Ikin, Texas, 57.

23 *Telegraph and Texas Register*, April 14, 1838.

24 MS. George W. Smyth Papers.

25 British Correspondence Concerning Texas, Ephraim Douglass Adams (ed), *Quarterly* XV, 223.

26 *Telegraph and Texas Register*, Jan. 13, 1838.

Several of our citizens have just returned from the up country and the far West, where they have been engaged since the opening of the land office, in locating their lands. They bring the most flattering accounts of the emigration which is now pouring into the interior with a rapidity altogether unparalled in the settlement of the country. The new comers we understand are nearly all farmers, and are now making extensive preparations to cultivate the soil. The Colorado, up to the base of the mountains, is alive with the opening of new plantations, and towns and villages seem to be springing up spontaneously along its banks.[27]

On November 11, 1840 Adolphus Sterne of Nacogdoches wrote in his diary: "Several strangers in Town today, Emigration pours in, en masse," and a few weeks later he wrote "Fryday the 27th...Emigrants literaly pouring in."[28]

As might readily be supposed, some of the people who came to Texas expected to find a kind of Utopia; they made the tedious journey only to be disillusioned when coming in contact with the grim realities of frontier life. Others, wholly unsuited to take up residence in a pioneering community, soon developed a strong distaste for Texas and returned to their former abodes. Bollaert has this class in mind when he writes:

I went to see Count de —— with whom I had come [as] a fellow passenger from England. He had located himself and family temporarilly about 10 miles from Houston up the Bayou. I found them all in a most miserable plight all down with 'Chills and fever.' Sickness had

---

27 Ernest William Winkler, The Seat of Government of Texas, in *Quarterly*, X, 208, cites Matagorda Bulletin, March 7, 1838.

28 Adolphus Sterne, H. Smither (ed), Diary of Adolphus Sterne, *Quarterly* XXXI, 65.

brought on disgust & they talk of returning to France. I fear that this instance of failure is that my worthy friend did not know how to choose his ground [locate]. The picture that presented itself was distressing, people brought up in the luxeries of Paris and full of intelligence were here seen utterly helpless. Such like people have come to this country from all parts of the globe; they fail—they get disgusted—return to their native homes and curse Texas.[29]

Most of the people, however, were more fortunate than the Count. Such was Mr. Ashbel Smith, a man of a well-to-do family, accustomed to the comforts of a North Carolina home, and therefore one whose antecedents inclined him to set an ordinary if not a high standard of living. When taking up residence, Mr. Smith realized that the new country did not afford him all the comforts and conveniences of a well established community, but he was nevertheless well satisfied from the beginning.[30] He got along well and after an interval wrote:

I am laying the foundation of a large fortune.—Tell Mr. Kincaid that I am determined to urge you...to come to this country, altho, I know it will be of no use nor avail.— My expenses here are enormous, for I live in the best style, but I make clear over and above all expenses more in one year, than I can in Carolina in half a dozen. Of this I will convince you when we meet. Besides my position in Society is the most desirable.[31]

---

29 Bollaert, Manuscript, 1, 148.
30 Ashbel Smith to George Smith, MS. Ashbel Smith Papers.
31 Smith to Kincaid, MS. Ashbel Smith Papers.

That the early Texans considered Texas as their home, and that from the very beginning they were ready to defend it and its people, is evidenced by the patriotism they displayed. This sentiment of cooperation must have appealed strongly to the English visitor Bollaert since he makes very many striking references to it in his journal. Bollaert was staying at the Tremont Hotel, Galveston, in March, 1842, when one of the prisoners in the Santa Fe expedition, who had been successful in making his escape, arrived and gave reports about the condition of his less fortunate brethren still in captivity. The citizens of Galveston, upon hearing the news, held a public meeting at the Tremont Hotel to consider the possibility of aiding the prisoners. "Every proposal regarding the future welfare of the prisoners was carried. Public and private resources were to be used," and President Sam Houston was to be informed of the wishes of the people of Galveston.[32] The Englishman further records that there was so much excitement in the town that the court sessions were broken up abruptly and that the Chief Justice, the clerk, and the "Gentlemen of the Bar" were offering their services in favor of the distressed. Similar meetings were held in other communities of the Republic.[33]

Later in the year Bollaert again refers to the Santa Fe prisoners. Some of them had been liberated and returned to Texas in a most pitiable condition, most of them wretchedly clad. We read in Bollaert's diary of how they were aided by the people of Galveston:

> Sept. 21 – There was a Meeting this Evening to procure means to clothe the poor fellows. Everyone ransacked his wardrobe…for this purpose.
>
> Sept. 23 – The Santa Fe prisoners…each got well clothed and appeared pretty comfortable.

---

32 Bollaert, Manuscript, I, 34-37.
33 Ibid., 44.

> Sept. 29 – Meeting held by the citizens of Galveston; thanks were voted to —— for their humane exertions in favor of the Santa Fe prisoners.[34]

This same sentiment was manifested by the Texans when the Mexicans invaded San Antonio in 1842. Bollaert was at Copano at the time and was singularly impressed at the scarcity of men in the settlement. This oddity was explained when he learned that the men had gone to the defense of San Antonio when the first news of the invasion reached them, leaving the women and children at home.[35]

Many untoward things happened during the early years, and if the citizens really wanted to build a worthwhile Republic, they had to be constantly on the watch for the forces that tended to disrupt the peace of the community. Genuine devotedness was essential. Frontier journalists, forced by circumstances to confine themselves to news of a local nature, usually chronicled these events. Accounts of patriotism like the one given here from a Houston paper point out how zealously the interests of the country were protected:

> A company under the command of Capt. Reuben Ross, left this City a few days since for the West. We under stand that they are to be mounted and are destined for the protection and assistance of the civil authorities of the counties of San Patricio, Refugio and Victoria against banditti composed of Americans, Mexicans and Indians who have for some time committed the most desperate outrages upon the Rio Grande Traders.[36]

The colonists therefore, for mutual protection, had frequent

---

34 Ibid., I, 179.

35 Ibid., 55.

36 *Telegraph and Texas Register*, July 17, 1839.

occasion to associate with one another; the arrival of new settlers from the States with news about their former homes and friends also encouraged association; furthermore, the ever-pressing needs of a pioneer community made the settler go to his neighbor for the necessities that he lacked. This fellowship developed into a hospitality that became one of the outstanding characteristics of the people. Visitors to Texas wrote about this hospitality in their letters; contemporary writers usually stressed it in their histories and pamphlets; and the early settlers in writing their recollections and memoirs in later years liked to linger and multiply examples of this distinguishing trait of the frontier and so leave us under the impression that it was one of the most pleasant, and at the same time one of the most notable traits of the people.

The immigrant came in touch with this hospitality even before he settled. He found the settler ever-ready to share his provisions with the traveler, and so it happened that the Texans living along the routes most frequented by immigrants left an imprint of their kindness on the hearts of the travelers, and have gone down on record for the charity they dispensed. The Huling home at Zavala was noted for this kind of hospitality. Situated in the extreme eastern part of Texas, it was frequented by many who crossed the border and went westward. Mrs. Huling was known as a generous hostess, and was often blessed by the many who partook of her charity and shared the shelter of her home.[37]

Gray, describing his travels through Texas, recalls many kindnesses that were shown to him when he stopped at various places as an unannounced guest. He tells in particular of stopping at the widow Anderson's one night long after dark, only to be followed by a foot traveler, who partook of their supper.[38] Lubbock, in recalling early events, notes that "really it was an exception when we sat down to the table without company;" and he assures us "no traveler

---

37 Adele B. Looscan, Elizabeth B. Huling. A Texas Pioneer, *Quarterly*, XI, 08.

38 W. F. Gray, *From Virginia to Texas in 1835*, (Houston 1909) 105.

ever stopped without having his horse and himself taken care of free of charge."[39] J. H. Herndon writes that in 1848, he "went to several cottages at Clopper's bar between Galveston and Houston and found the inmates very hospitable."[40] Still another immigrant gives his impressions of Texas as he knew it during the years following his entrance (1834):

> The habits and customs of the people at that time were few and simple. The hospitality of the people could scarcely be equaled. At every house there was always a pot of coffee, and no matter at what hour of the day you happened to call you would be handed a cup. You could travel all over the country, and it would cost you no board.[41]

Lockhart expresses practically the same sentiments when he tells of the early days on the Brazos; he adds, moreover, that whether one's host was poor or not he was always "the soul of hospitality."[42] The Reverend McCalla summed up his sentiments in this extravagant way:

> While my breath lasts, I trust that my heart will beat with gratitude to God, and gratitude to them the citizens of Galveston, for the treatment received at their hands, and at the hands of their fellow citizens throughout the republic.[43]

The hospitality extended to Bollaert by some of the citizens of Galveston on his arrival in that city made a very favorable impression on him, and he has left an account of it in these words:

---

39 Lubbock, *Six Decades in Texas*, 123.
40 J. H. Herndon, MS. Diary of a Trip from Kentucky to Texas, University of Texas, Austin.
41 Recollections of S. F. Sparks, *Quarterly*, XII, 78.
42 Wallis, *Sixty Years on the Brazos*, 14.
43 Rev. W. L. McCalla, *Adventures in Texas*, (Philadelphia, 1841), 17.

When at last I got into an avenue something like a street...I proceeded [to a hotel]...and saw several persons...round a stove. I entered when it was soon perceived that I was a 'Stranger.' I approached the fire to light a Segar, I was politely offered a seat—when the Acting Man opened the conversation. 'Stranger I guess you came [on] the Brig today?' I replied in the affirmative...and although the Boarding House was full of people The 'Stranger' was accommodated.[44]

This happened on the day Bollaert arrived in Texas, and truly it indicated the kind of treatment he could expect from the Texans. His journal contains numerous references to it, but only a few need be cited. Speaking of Mr. James Power, empresario and old settler of Live Oak Point: "He received us most hospitably. Had 'Beefs' (Oxen) killed for us, supplied us with Milk, fish etc."[45] Again, stopping at a farm a short distance below Seguin, on his way to San Antonio: "Noon'd [had dinner]...very pretty lass undertook to supply our wants."[46] And again, "The rest of the time I remained in Matagorda passed pleasantly indeed, and I shall ever cherish a grateful remembrance for unremitting attentions and kindness."[47]

The Texans did not confine their attentions and services to immigrants and visitors. The following passage shows the extent to which they assisted each other:

It was sometimes necessary for my husband to be away from home, and during his absences I found the neighbors always ready to do anything they could for me. I wish I could emphasize this feature of our early Texas life;

---

44 Bollaert, Manuscript, I, 19.
45 Ibid., I, 53.
46 Ibid., 73.
47 Ibid., 93.

the spirit of helpfulness and friendly fellowship that always prevailed. It was one of the
best of the good things of the new country. We
were all strangers thrown together, willing to
lend or borrow as the case might be. Anything
one had was at the disposal of the others. If we
had no meat we felt no hesitancy in going to a
neighbor for it—if he had any.

To the first wedding to which I was invited in
Texas I carried the dress in which the bride was
married, and the plates from which we ate the
wedding dinner. During my husband's first
long absence from home—three months—I do
not recall that I stayed more than that number
of nights alone, the family which had had the
wedding always supplied me with one of the
girls for company...In sickness our neighbors
were always ready to do all they could to help.[48]

The hospitality of the Texans tended to develop a good
fellowship, gayety, and lightheartedness that made each
regard all as equals, and expressed itself in a singular disregard for rank. Pioneer life never considers a man's past
accomplishments; it is based essentially on what a man is
and what he can do. This spirit prevailed in the Texas
communities as it does in all new lands. Oddly enough it
expressed itself in a burlesque way, and hence we see titles,
military and civil, bestowed promiscuously on all the inhabitants. It would have been quite impossible to live a year in
the Republic without being addressed as general, major,
captain, judge, doctor, or squire. Bollaert, after traveling a
bit, gave up all hope of maintaining his "simple cognomen
of Mister" and expected to "die a martyr to the prevailing
taste of the sovereign people."[49]

48 Reminiscences of Frances Cooke Lipscomb, wife of Isaac Van Zandt. MS. Isaac Van
Zandt Letters, 1835-1847.
49 Bollaert, Manuscript, I, 106.

In fact this particular habit of the Texans made such an impression on him that he wrote a few verses about it—verses which, as he said, would appropriately serve as an epitaph for the man whose many friends should each contribute a part. The composite would read:

> The General died a true believer
> The Colonel liv'd "a gay deceiver"
> The Major died an easy death
> The Captain's gone for want of breath.
> The Judge is freed from worldly pains
> Peace be to the Doctor's manes
> The squire died of persecution
> Which hath not ceased with dissolution.[50]

Perhaps in exchanging kindnesses the Texans lingered with their neighbors to discuss their affairs, and as the conversation lagged they whittled sticks to amuse themselves; perhaps, in the long evenings after work, they whittled and thought out their problems in a solitary way; maybe the fact that they were always equipped with a bowie knife was a constant temptation for them to make an art of whittling—whatever the reason, the early Texans from all contemporary accounts were "desperate whittlers of sticks." The practice was so common that one visitor remarked that a Texan could be expected to take out his knife and start whittling as soon as you entered into conversation with him.[51]

These were the Texans. These were the men who built up the Republic to a point sufficiently high to permit it to enter the Union of States, without being obliged to go through the territorial stage. This is sufficient evidence that they built well; that they also built extensively must be concluded when the affairs of the Republic are surveyed both at the beginning and at the end of its existence. The growth of both Galveston and Houston is typical of the progress made.

---

50 Bollaert, Manuscript, I, 106.

51 Maillard, *Texas*, 21.1.

Early Galveston is pictured to us in a history written during the existence of the Republic: "In 1836, there was hardly one arrival in a month of shipping at the port. In 1837, there were but seven houses on the island. In May 1839, there were thirty sail vessels in the harbour at one time; three steamers plying regularly between it and New Orleans."[52]

William Bollaert had this account of Galveston with him while he was in that city. He quotes the above passage in his manuscript and then completes the picture up to February 1842, pointing out that in the intervening years the growth was striking. In 1842 the population seemed more fixed, the building of houses more continuous, trade with New Orleans more brisk, and the entire scene presented a view of greater activity and bustle.[53]

Sam Maverick had occasion to travel through Houston several times in his many trips to and from San Antonio. On December 29, 1838, he writes: "It is astonishing to see the great improvement in Houston; Merchants all increasing their stock and making [this place] quite a busy mart."[54]

The citizens of the Republic of Texas struggled through privations and hardships to make a living and build homes for themselves and their descendents. It was a task that the Spaniards vainly planned, and one that the Mexicans utterly failed to accomplish. How well the Anglo-American pioneers surmounted the difficulties that had checked other nations, and how well they succeeded in building their own nation may be concluded from a contemporary account:

> With every prospect to discourage them...
> [their efforts were] crowned with the most
> complete success, & in the short space of eight
> years, have transformed into an abode of intel-
> ligence, industry and prosperity, a land which

---

52 William Kennedy, *Texas: the Rise, Progress & Prospects of the Republic of Texas.* (London, 1841), 2 vols., II, 407-408.

53 Bollaert, Manuscript, I, 28-29.

54 Sam to Mary A. Maverick, MS. Maverick Papers.

under the dominion of other people claiming to be civilized, had failed to give any evidences of emerging from barbarism, and only began to show signs of improvement on the introduction of the race who now possess it.

Texas which up to within a few years of the revolution was only known, even to the wisest Statesman of the American continent, from the uncertain & ignorant savages, as the lurking places of pirates and outlaws, now engages the attention of the most civilized nations...

Agriculture blesses with abundance the plains that were desolate & unproductive; the axe rings in the forest; the towns resound with the hum of industry, where eight years ago man had no habitation, & the reign of silence & solitude was scarcely ever broken by the voice of a human being. The harbor of Galveston, which then was only known as the rendezvous of pirates, is now white with the sails & gay with the flags of Europe & America, lured hither by the lucrative commerce, awakened by the industry of the hardy possessors of the soil.

Agriculture, arts, trade, learning & religion are steadily advancing, & show on every hand, as the evidence of their onward march, plantations, farms, & luxuriant fields, rising towns, & busy work shops; ports & bays white with canvas, rivers navigated by swift-moving steamers, academies of learning; temples filled with pious people, and pulpits from which learned, gifted & devout men impart the blessings of religion.[55]

---

55 Bollaert, Manuscript, II, 218.

Pole Cabins, Yellow Fever & Jerked Beef:
The Basics

The early Texas pioneers were a hardy people. The great majority realized that only by hard work would they reap the good fortune they so ardently desired. Accordingly they began work immediately upon arrival, labored long and hard, and muttered not. Usually their first care was the erection of a house. There were few good houses built in the first years; building material was scarce and high priced, and the houses constructed, usually by the immigrant with the help of friendly neighbors, were mere shelters, hardly deserving of the name. The majority of the houses, excluding those in the towns, were simply constructed, built of logs, clapboards, and rough sawed planks.[1]

Conditions in the backwoods were especially poor. Inhabitants had a roof over their heads and little else. "Many of the houses were made by setting poles in the ground ...and boarding them up with split pine boards."[2] The entire affair, made of logs, was small: "one room harbored the whole family and comers and goers;"[3] and sometimes it did not even have a window. When air and light were wanted, a board was knocked off. These houses had floors made of rough boards laid on the ground, sometimes not extending under the bed.[4] At times they lacked even this rough surface and the ground had to serve as the base of all domestic operations.[5] Mrs. Isaac Van Zandt gives us a good idea of what these early homes were like:

> Our first houses [in 1839] were...pole cabins
> with the cracks chinked with split out lumber,
> daubed with clay, mortar and sometimes boards

1 Lubbock, *Six Decades in Texas*, 54.

2 Allen's Reminiscences of Texas 1838-42, William S. Red (ed), *Quarterly* XVIII, 294.

3 Lucy A. Erath, Memoirs, *Quarterly* XXVI, 223.

4 Lubbock, *Six Decades in Texas*, 54.

5 Wallis, *Sixty Years on the Brazos*, 91.

pinned on with wooden pins…Clapboard doors hung on wooden hinges…The chimneys were of sticks and dirt…The houses had split out puncheon floors when there were any kind at all.6

Most of the pioneers, however, could boast of dwellings somewhat better than the backwoods type. But at best their homes were crudely built; totally lacking comforts or conveniences and still strictly primitive structures. They at least had windows and plank floors and rock chimneys and fireplaces.7 Nor were the furnishings of these early dwellings superior to their surroundings. Most of the articles were of the roughest construction. Tables were made of green lumber from trees; chairs were built out of round sticks and cross-pieces, and seated with deer skin or rawhide. The beds, as tight as the face of a drum, were made of skins which were used without covering of any kind. Where mattresses were used, they were of Spanish moss, corn husks, prairie grass, etc.8 Doctor Lockhart tells us of his early surroundings as he remembers them:

> The table, chairs, and bedsteads were usually homemade. If the head of the house possessed any mechanical genius the good lady could move her furniture occasionally; if not, the bedsteads were made by boring an auger hole in the side of the house, a pole was driven into it, extending out the width of the bed, a forked stick was driven in the ground for the end to rest on. This operation was repeated at the other end and a pole laid on, thus making a scaffold for bedding, and the job was completed.9

---

6 MS. Isaac Van Zandt Letters.

7 Lucy A. Erath, Memoirs, *Quarterly* XXVI, 223.

8 N. Doran Maillard, *Texas*, 223.

9 Wallis, *Sixty Years on the Brazos*, 91.

Houses of this type evidently lacked even the elementary comforts of life and did little to shelter the inmates from the weather. The howling Texas winds of the winter months had an annoying way of whistling through the many cracks in the poorly constructed walls "thus placing the small room still more at the mercy of the icy norther."[10] Conditions were not much better in summer, as few homes had screens to protect the dwellers against the vicious sting of the mosquito.[11]

Some of the most important men in the Republic had lived in these rude houses. General Moseley Baker, called one of Houston's "first citizens" lived in a "small house built of clapboards."[12] Even President Houston lived for years in "a small log house consisting of two rooms and a passage through, after the Southern fashion."[13]

It must be remembered that these dwellings were built by the immigrant immediately upon arrival, when circumstances forced him to be grateful for any kind of shelter. The progressive pioneer was not, however, content to live the rest of his days amidst such primitive conditions; accordingly, at odd moments, and whenever an opportunity presented itself, he improved the building. "The hewn logs were covered with weather boards, the interior walls ceiled [sic] and papered, a second story was added, and it was protected on three sides with wide galleries on both stories."[14] Gradually, therefore, the log houses took on a more presentable appearance and the dwellings became habitable.

It would be false, however, to create the impression that most of the homes went through the log stage. In the towns and cities where material and labor were available, some very

---

10 Erath, Memoirs, *Quarterly* XXVI, 223.

11 Bollaert, Manuscript, II, 94.

12 Lubbock, *Six Decades in Texas*, 58.

13 Ibid., 53.

14 Adele B. Looscan, Harris County, 1822-1845; *Quarterly* XXXII, 369.

worthwhile houses were constructed from the very start. A saw mill was introduced into Texas as early as 1830[15] and with machine-cut lumber it was possible to make homes quite attractive. It is evidently to homes of this kind that Mrs. Holley refers when she writes from Galveston in 1840 that there were "some very pretty houses...of Grecian architecture, one story, with columns [in] front & windows to the floor like glass doors, all painted white & having a neat white paling around them."[16] When houses of this type were set in towns that were planned with wide streets and alleys, and where provisions were made for public squares and everything arranged in good taste, the effect was not unlike that of a present day city.[17] There was a decided difference between living in such surroundings and in the untracked wastelands of the backwoods.

Those who came to Texas in the early years soon found out that life was many-sided and complicated, that the needs of a pioneering community were many, and that to succeed meant hard work from morning to night. That there was no place for the laggard and loafer was soon evident. Life was essentially a struggle for existence, a struggle that by no means ended with the construction of a dwelling—in fact, the striving began only then. The problems that presented themselves were as numerous as they were varied— they dealt with every phase of existence that might be encountered from the time of infancy to the grave; they usually had to be solved at once, since to shirk them was only to delay them; but to solve them required versatility. Some idea of the nature of the problems and how the Texan solved them may be got from the reminiscences of Mrs. Lipscomb:

------

15 Lewis Newton, Herbert Gambrell, *A Social and Political History of Texas,* (Dallas, 1932), 124.

16 Mary A. Holley to Mrs. Wm. Brand Nov. 12, 1840, Mary Austin Holley Letters, 1808-1846, Photostat, University of Texas, Austin.

17 W. J. Sandusky to H. J. Jewett, Aug. 1839, *Lamar Papers*, III, 91.

When our need for things was pressing, we usually found a way for making them. One time Mr. Van Zandt needed a saddle and he made it, having only a drawing knife with which to fashion the saddle-tree from a dead sassafras which he cut down for the purpose. His shoes were gone and he could get no others. He bought some red leather, made a last, and manufactured some very respectable shoes, which he wore to Memphis. One night Matthew Cartwright came to spend the night with us. We had no candles for the supper table, so my husband scraped up some tallow, made a wick, squeezed the tallow round it, then rolled it over and over until it was straight, and we had a very good candle. After we went to Harrison county there was a new baby, and no cradle for him. The saw and drawing-knife were called on, and a complete bed was made.[18]

A glance at the illuminating journal of Daniel Hartzo, a farmer in the Jefferson area, further shows to what extent life was self-sustaining. On November 22, 1841, he wrote in his diary that he had begun making a wheel. On November 29, 1841, he made a coffin, December 1, 1841, he "maid a reel," while on January 8, 1842, he recounts that he "hude puncheons." On February 3, 1842, Hartzo "grained deer skins," and on April 7, 1842 he "maid a chern." His task for May 16, 1842 was to construct a cradle. On June 11, 1842 he tells about making a bucket. On September 27, 1842, he "maid a Pump Auger," and on October 27, 1842, he "maid an ox yoke." On July 25, 1843, the versatile Hartzo "maid a pair of Shoes." On February 5, 1844, he "maid a Cart tongue," and the next day he "maid a Cart body."[19]

---

18 MS. Isaac Van Zandt Letters.
19 MS. Diary of Daniel Hartzo, Feb. 1, 1841-Dec. 31, 1846, University of Texas, Austin.

It is evident that the pioneer had to be a jack-of-all-trades to survive the many demands. The men who succeeded shaped the history of the Republic; those who failed fell by the wayside, returned home, or stayed in the country only to follow the line of least resistance. It is in the former that we are interested. Besides these domestic and agricultural demands that presented themselves at frequent intervals, the immigrant was often perplexed by the ever-present necessity of providing food and clothing for himself and his family.

Supplying food for the family was largely a domestic task. Most of it was procured at home; the variety of the meals depended on the skill of the head of the family either as a hunter or as a gardener. Corn was the staple food of most of the people; in one form or another it was the main dependence in Texas.[20] The wealth and advantages of certain sections of the vast lands of the country were often calculated by the corn that was already growing there or that it was possible to raise.[21] Because of the thousands of fat beeves that roamed the prairies, meat found a conspicuous place in the diet. Along with cattle naturally went plenty of good dairy products — "milk, curds, clabber, and butter."[22] The difficulty of preserving the meat was solved by a process known as "jerking beef." The beef would be cut into long thin strips and sun dried. School children often took some of this in their lunch boxes, and it was the favorite food of the men when leaving home for a journey of several days.[23] But not only was the meat "jerked" to prepare for long marches, but sometimes kitchen doors were supplied with iron hooks upon which newly purchased steaks were hung and dried in the hot sun. There was a little more variety for those people who lived around the gulf; fish, turtle and

---

20 Abigail Curlee. The History of a Texas Slave Plantation 1831-1863, *Quarterly* XXVI, 99.

21 W. H. Sandusky to H. J. Jewett, Aug. 1839. *Lamar Papers* III, 91.

22 Lubbock, *Six Decades in Texas*, 123.

23 MS. Memoirs of Mary A. Maverick, 46. I am indebted for the use of these Memoirs, as well as for the use of the Diary of Mary A. Maverick to Mrs. Norval J. Welsh, San Antonio.

oysters were easily obtainable and frequently found a place in the menu.[24]

Naturally housekeeping under such a system was not a complicated matter, but it must be remembered that it was a sort of hand-to-mouth existence. The chances of starvation were slim, but there was often an actual shortage of food and supplies, due to varying conditions such as particular seasons or unusual demands. This is indicated by an announcement in a Houston newspaper:

> Important to Emigrants—The crowd of travellers on the road between Nacogdoches and Washington has lately been so great that provisions have become quite scarce along the whole route. The emigrating families therefore, who are journeying westward will do well to provide themselves near Nacogdoches or San Augustine, with a sufficiency of provisions to supply them their wants until they can reach the Brazos.[25]

People living in cities and depending in part on the local merchants for their supplies found the prices of all commodities and foodstuffs very high, and quite often these were hard to get at any price. As early as December 18, 1836, Clopper writes: "Provision is very scarce and hard to get. Flour is now selling at Lynch's at $18 per Bbl., and I am told it is 20 on the Brazos. Sugar 20cts per lb."[26] Lubbock, a merchant in Houston in 1837, made a good profit by selling flour at $30.00 a barrel and coffee at 25 cents a pound.[27] An examination of the price lists of commodities in Houston and Galveston in 1838 and 1839 reveals: Flour $30.00 bbl.; coffee 25¢ lb.; bacon 25¢ lb.; cheese 50¢ lb.; eggs $2.00 doz.;

---

24 W. Roberts to Lamar, July 12, 1838, *Lamar Papers* II, 183.

25 *Telegraph and Texas Register*, March 3, 1838.

26 A. M. Clopper to Nicholas Clopper, Dec. 18, 1834. Clopper Correspondence 1834 to 1838, *Quarterly* XIII, 137.

27 Lubbock, *Six Decades in Texas*, 48.

butter $1.00 lb.; rice 25¢ lb.; whiskey $2.00 gallon.[28] These prices continued high throughout the time of the Republic; as late as December, 1845, James Addison writes that "goods, groceries and in fact everything except coffee is very high. Flour is selling at $12 per Barrel and coffee at 12¢ per pound [and] everything according[ly]."[29]

The people living in the less settled districts, especially in the West, far removed from the ports of entry and from the transportation routes, such as they were, were particularly pressed for supplies; in most cases supplies could not be procured at all. The Houston paper comments on this in 1838, and offers it as an explanation as to why the congressmen "have a singular aversion to visit the western districts."[30] Conditions evidently did not improve a great deal when the capital was moved to Austin, for as late as 1845 Dr. Moses Johnson wrote to his wife and asked her to send some quinine as he was out and there was none to be had at the capital.[31]

With existing conditions anything might have been expected, and so it is not surprising to notice that Jesse Hord records in his diary: "We traveled all day through an uninhabited pine country, arriving at a tavern on the river Neches. A tavern? Yes; one without meat, coffee or vegetables—milk out of the question." Hord adds, however, that more travelers arrived at the inn, and that the proprietor had a hog killed and prepared for the guests, so that it was possible for them to eat a fried pork supper at ten o'clock.[32]

Naturally the blame for the scarcity of supplies was placed on the store-keepers; really the cause lay deeper. The

———

28 James E. Winston. Notes on Commercial Relations Between New Orleans and Texan Ports, 1838-1839. *Quarterly* XXXIV, 105.

29 J. H. Addison to O. M. Addison, Dec. 8, 1845, MS. Addison Papers.

30 *Telegraph and Texas Register*, July 7, 1838.

31 Moses Johnson to Olivia Johnson Aug. 2.2, 1845, Moses Johnson Correspondence, 1834-1852, Photostat, University of Texas, Austin.

32 Rev. Homer S. Thrall. *A Brief History of Methodism in Texas* (Nashville, Term. 1889), 56.

businessman, with an eye to profits, was always ready to equip his place of business with all the necessaries, but it must be remembered that this was the frontier, and therefore, all his efforts were often in vain. Moses Evans, a Washington merchant, wrote to General Hunt at Galveston on May 21, 1845:

> I have not received any word from you since you left this place in relation to the Groceries that you were to purchase for me, if you have purchased them you will please send them by the first opportunity as I stand in great need of them at this time. Congress will soon meet and I wish to have them at this place during the session...[33]

Evans asked Hunt to use his land certificates and exchange them for the groceries, but evidently no groceries were available, for Evans wrote again the following week:

> I Would be Glad If that you Would Send me Some Groceries as I am in particular Need...I wish you to Send Me Brandy Whiskey Wines & Cigars of the best quality all and every thing that you think would Come under my line of business, Brown & Loaf sugar &c...[34]

This shortage can best be explained by the irregular shipping and also by an irregular demand, one which could not be gauged accurately since there was no way of estimating the number of immigrants or the other variable factors that to this day present problems in well-established communities. Even commodities that the retail merchant got from the farmers and plantation owners were obtained quite irregularly. An examination of the records of a slave plantation reveals that eggs (by the keg), butter, pecans, tallow,

33 Moses Evans to M. Hunt. May 21, 1845. MS. Hunt Papers, 1838-1848, Texas State Library, Austin.
34 Evans to Hunt, May 25, 1845, MS. Hunt Papers.

soap, chickens, turkeys and various other domesticated fowls and meats, were sold to the stores. But the sales were never in large quantities nor were they made at regular intervals.[35]

Whenever a merchant was fortunate enough to procure supplies he usually inserted an advertisement to that effect in the newspaper. The notice frequently listed the entire stock offered for sale. Anthony Blandon's Brazoria store is typical:

> Super fine and fancy clothing, saddlery, sugar, coffee, flour, corn, Havana segars, rice, tea, candles, rope, bagging, cheese, biscuits, crackers, pilot bread, tongues, hams, bacon, oil, codfish, madeira, port, claret, and, other superior wines, brandy, fruits, syrup, pickles, cordials, rum, gin, whiskey, shoes, hats, bridles and stirrups.[36]

Again it must be pointed out that there were some people in the Republic who, on account of their position in society, and because they were financially independent, could live a life of comparative ease and comfort; these people were not inconvenienced by the general dearth of supplies and provisions. It is from the pen of one of these that we get a picture of life as it was led in the McKinney home at Quintana:

> We passed a day or two with Mrs. McKenney at Quintana [Mrs Holley wrote to her daughter]. Mr. Toby was there from New Orleans — & Mr. Williams, just from the States — It is very pleasant there — was delightful riding on the beach — where 5 miles of our road lay…They live remarkably well there, having everything they want from New Orleans — a

35 Curlee, Slave Plantation, *Quarterly*, XXVI, 103.
36 *Telegraph and Texas Register* March 28, 1837.

brig and schooner came while we were there
& [they] are constantly coming.[37]

In providing clothes for himself and his family, the pioneer faced a problem greatly similar to that of obtaining food. The people were forced to practice all sorts of economies; there was not a great deal of money available, and these were frontier conditions, so that a great many of the colonists made their own clothes at home.[38] The loom and spinning wheel were ordinary household objects, and the style and perfection of the individual garments depended on the ability of the womenfolk. Sometimes the outer garments were made out of buckskin, and it was not an unusual sight to see men attired in this fashion. The women also dressed very plainly; they wore calico if it was obtainable; if not they had to be content with homespun.[39]

"Store clothes" in the shape of manufactured garments were rare indeed. An examination of a list of merchandise offered to the public by the A. G. Compton Store of Houston, one of the best stocked stores of the Republic, reveals that the retailer offered a great variety of goods that the individual would have had difficulty in making at home, such as "dancing pumps, ladies' and misses' dancing pumps and walking shoes," or "ladies' black, white, and colored kid, silk, cotton and woolen gloves"; stockings were likewise offered in all varieties. The only manufactured garment, or ready-to-wear article of common use, that Compton had for sale was "merino shirts" — and this was an exceptionally well-supplied store. However, every variety of cloth was offered: "brown and white domestic cotton, colored American cambrics, black and colored merinoes, calicoes, ginghams, crepes, silks."[40]

---

37 Holley to Brand, Feb. 8, 1838. MS. Holley Letters.
38 Wallis, *Sixty Years on the Brazos*, 90.
39 Ibid., 91.
40 *Telegraph and Texas Register*, Dec. 22, 1838.

The wardrobe of the early Texan was not confined entirely to homemade clothes. Balls, parties, weddings, and other gala celebrations were always graced by the Texan attired in his best. At these gatherings "the styles were somewhat varied according to the period at which the wearer migrated,"[41] but the clothes were of good material. Elaborate velvet suits, with highly ornamented boots, fluffed waistcoats, flowing ties and scarves of purple silk or checked cotton were in evidence.[42] Lubbock describes the costumes of some of the people who attended a ball given in Houston in 1837:

> He was of course the hero of the day [speaking of President Houston] and his dress on this occasion was unique and somewhat striking. His ruffled shirt, scarlet cassimere waistcoat and suit of black silk velvet, corded with gold, was admirably adapted to set off his fine, tall figure; his boots, with short red tops, were laced and folded down in such a way as to reach but little above the ankles, and were finished at the heels with silver spurs. The spurs were, of course, quite a useless adornment, but they were in those days so commonly worn as to seem almost a part of the boots...Mrs. Baker's dress of white satin, with black lace overdress, corresponded in elegance with that of her escort, [Houston] and the dresses of most of the other ladies were likewise rich and tasteful. Some wore white mull, with satin trimmings; others were dressed in white and colored satins, but naturally in so large an assembly, gathered from many different places, there was great variety in the quality of costumes.[43]

---

41 Noah Smithwick, *Evolution of a State*, (Austin, 1900), 153.
42 C. F. Schmidt to Viktor Friederich Bracht, a Texas Pioneer, *Quarterly*, XXXV 288.
43 Lubbock, *Six Decades in Texas*, 59, cites *Ladies Messenger*.

The shortcomings of frontier food and clothes were often considerable, but even in their most acute form they could be endured with a light heart by the settlers who were prepared for hardships. The same cannot be said of sickness. The most common form of sickness was fever, both congestive and bilious. The people living in the bottomlands along the rivers, particularly the Guadalupe, Colorado, Brazos and Trinity, and the inhabitants of seacoast cities such as Galveston and Houston, were particularly subject to these devastating fevers.[44] The maladies came at intervals, and naturally their severity could not be foretold. That they were severe is beyond doubt. In October, 1839, Wilkens wrote:

> Houston at present is very sickly...there is scarcely a day passes that we have not six or eight funerals...the doctors have come to the conclusion that we have yellow fever here— also at Galveston.[45]

A less severe siege of fevers had been experienced by the Houston citizens two years previously:

> Persons recently from Houston state that the city presents rather a gloomy appearance and worse in prospect. At the time our informant left there was much sickness, principally fevers—of which there had been cases of yellow conjestive and billious.[46]

Generally speaking, the western section of Texas, being at a higher elevation and further removed from the marshy lands, escaped these fevers. This diminished risk of disease was one of the advantages considered in 1838 by the commissioners appointed to find a site for the permanent seat of

---

44 *Telegraph and Texas Register*, Sept. 20, 1843.

45 R. R. Wilkens to Lamar, Oct. 15, 1839, Lamar Papers III, 134.

46 Ernest Winkler, Seat of Government *Quarterly* X, 187, cites *The Matagorda Bulletin* for Oct. 25, 1837.

government, and it was not the least of the factors influenc-
ing their choice in favor of the western city of Austin.[47]

The struggle against sickness was rendered all the more
difficult because of the dearth of good physicians. The medical profession was not on the same high plane as it is today,
and so it frequently happened that the doctor, in addition to
his regular profession was "at the same time a small Planter
& Farmer."[48] Nor could competent service be expected
when the infirm, for one reason or another, could not per-
sonally consult a doctor. It is impossible to judge to what
extent people were forced to obtain their medical advice
through correspondence, but evidently there were very
many cases. In the correspondence of Dr. Ashbel Smith
many private professional letters of this type are filed.
Newspaper advertisements also contain references to the
practice: "Persons living in the country may by sending a
statement of their complaints have remedies forwarded to
any part of the country by making a remittance."[49]

This haphazard practice of medicine presented such
evident dangers that the legislature of the Republic considered ways of improving it. A real step forward was taken
when, on December 14, 1837, the government of the Republic passed a law regulating the medical profession. A board
of "Medical Censors" was created and empowered to exam-
ine all applicants and grant licenses to such as satisfactorily
gave evidence of their qualifications.[50]

This law undoubtedly improved the personnel of the
profession but it did not immediately act in favor of the
colonist. The service offered was more competent probably,
but the rates were still too high. Some idea of prices may be
gathered by examining the rates set down by the Medical
and Surgical Society of Houston:

––––––

47 *Telegraph and Texas Register*, April 21, 1838.
48 Bollaert, Manuscript, II, 183.
49 *Telegraph and Texas Register*, April A, 1837.
50 Kennedy, *Texas*, II, 415.

> When first called to a patient, the charge for
> one visit shall be five dollars. After nine
> o'clock, P. M., the charges for professional
> visits shall be doubled in all cases. For visits
> out of the limits of the city, an extra charge of
> one dollar a mile during the day, and two
> dollars a mile at night.[51]

Individuals coming to Texas from the more settled and better established communities were often adversely impressed. An Englishman wrote from Galveston in 1844: "Medical attendance is very expensive, and Nurses for the sick are difficult to be procured. For about twelve days' Medical attendance, Medicine, etc., during my illness...I had to pay above Sixty-five pounds Sterling."[52] The story is not entirely one-sided, however; the physician had his worries also. In a country that was not on a sound financial basis, and where there was an actual shortage of a circulating medium, anything might be expected in lieu of cash, and so it often happened that the doctor had to be content to take "cows & calves, horses, pigs, cotton etc., etc.," in exchange for his services.[53]

The profession was not without its noble souls. Occasionally a man was found who gave his services generously and gratuitously. Such a man was Doctor Wiedeman of San Antonio. A Russian by descent, a world traveler, and a linguist of note, Doctor Wiedeman settled in San Antonio in the forties and soon established an enviable reputation for devotedness and skillful attention to the sick and wounded.[54]

It has been pointed out that the large majority of the people in Texas had to struggle for their existence, that great efforts were put forth in the very beginning with the erection of a house, and that the striving did not end, but in a

51 Ibid.
52 British Correspondence Concerning Texas, *Quarterly*, XIX, 98.
53 Bollaert, Manuscript, II, 183.
54 Maverick, Memoirs, 32, 35.

sense really began only then. It has also been pointed out that there were some well-to-do people who led a life of ease—a rare set indeed in the early history of the Texas people—but interesting to us if for no other reason than to insist, by contrast, on the ordinary every day struggle of the majority. Bollaert, who had experience in dealing with people of leisure in England, gives a good first-hand account of the life of the leisure class in Galveston. Here is what he has to say:

> About sunrise prudent and judicious people will rise, prepare their toilette, clad themselves lightly, walk or work in the gardens, then ride or bathe on the seashore—at half past 7 A. M. bells may be heard ringing from the different Hotels; but in the tones of the 'Tremont' I can almost fancy the accompaniment to the words "Come to breakfast come!" The bells ring for about five minutes—stop short—the sluggards hold counsel of war with themselves, as to the propriety of "turning out." Now then, under the Tremont Verandah the boarders and others meet—words of recognition take place—some of the individuals may indulge in the "weed" *per humo* and *per masttcato.*
>
> A small bell is now rung when all take their places at the breakfast table—the ladies at the top. We all appear to suffer a little langor, the air is sultry—the sea breeze has not set in—we get this meal—which is a most excellent dejuener [sic] a la fourchette—retire, light the gentle Havana, discuss the politics of the day—a small quantity of whittling going on— but the quantity of wood thus destroyed will depend upon the excited state of the times &c.

Then those who have business attend to it —idlers may return to their rooms, read—and these idlers and visitors read a great deal— Bulwers last novel of Zanoni is here, this is a great favorite—then before dinner, billiards or nine pins may be played. At the bar of the Tremont lunch is laid—but to partake would be sinful, considering the excellent dinner that Capt. Seymore has in preparation, which is inhanced by the promptitude of his domestics.

"Come, come, to dinner come" the bell announces this most important of meals. We congregate again under the Verandah— impart to each other news etc.—probably take an iced mint-julip—the ice comes from U. States—a glass of Madera and bitters etc., etc. Then the little bell's inviting strain says "Dinner's on the table." In a moment the crowd of carnivore march for the dining room, where a dinner will be found prepared and arranged so as to meet our taste and wishes. Moreover one may enjoy a bottle of wine as the duties are low. Generally speaking they do not sit long at table—but sometimes a few of the jovial ones huddle together, and oftimes a few songs are heard. Not many of my Texas friends sing, but they appear very fond of singing and music.

Towards 4 or 5 o'clock pairties [sic] are made to go fishing on the beach with the seine—or a gallop on the prairie till dark—when "come, come, to supper come" is the signal to prepare to this meal—it is generally a teasupper—a quiet smoke in the Verandah—Long chats— and then each one off to some evening party or or other—where if there be no dancing there is music and singing — pretty good hours are kept—but it does not require much pursua-sion [sic] to sit for an hour or two in the cool of the evening, sup a mint-julip—touch a guitar and sing the song most loved.[55]

---

55 Bollaert, Manuscript, I, 30.

The Teacher, The Preacher & The Con:
Cultural Influences

Education was a subject that had interested the citizens of Texas for a good many years previous to the establishment of the Republic. That the Mexican government utterly neglected to provide for a system of education, and that the people were dissatisfied as a result, was evident as early as 1832. At that time the Texans, assembled in convention, officially complained to the Mexican government about this neglect, and insisted that it should be remedied.[1] But the government did not take action, and conditions remained the same for several years.

The people however did not lose interest in the subject and as soon as they had control of their own affairs they demonstrated that their former interest had been genuine. When the Constitution was framed in 1836, education was provided for by making it a duty of Congress, "as soon as circumstances will permit," to provide by legislative acts for a general system of education.

The first years of the Republic were trying ones, and the legislators, beset with many problems, did not establish a system. Nothing was accomplished until Mirabeau B. Lamar became president in 1838 and recommended educational legislation in his first message to Congress. He suggested to set aside part of the vast public lands as a permanent endowment for the cause of education; this could be done without inconvenience to the government or the people, and in so doing the "foundation of a great moral and intellectual edifice" would be laid. Should the legislators fail to make some such suitable appropriation at that time, Lamar said, and defer it until the public domain passed from the hands of the Republic, then "the uneducated youths of Texas will constitute the living monument

---

1 Frederick Eby. *The Development of Education in Texas* (New York, 1925), 79.

of our neglect and remissness."[2] The President's recommendations were entrusted to a special committee for consideration. The committee reported that it was not feasible to institute, immediately, a general system of education, but nonetheless it recommended that part of the lands of the state be set aside to establish primary schools and colleges as soon as conditions would permit.[3] The committee's report met with general approval, and its provisions were enacted into law. The bill as passed provided: "That each county of this Republic shall have three leagues [13,284 acres] of land surveyed and set apart for the purpose of establishing a primary school or academy in said county."[4] This bill was amended later on, and additional leagues of land were set aside for educational purposes; still it was the wisdom and foresight of the original statute that was responsible for the ultimate establishment of the system of education.[5]

The working out of this law, passed in the hope that these land grants to the counties would result in the prompt erection of schools, proved a disappointment. Land was so abundant and cheap that funds for school purposes could not be obtained from the immediate sale of these lands, and therefore the counties did not take action.[6] Twenty months after the law was passed granting each county three leagues, not a single survey had been made. As late as 1855 only forty-one counties had surveyed their lands; twenty had made partial surveys and thirty-eight had made no effort whatsoever. And there is no evidence that the counties that did make the surveys used the lands for the establishment of schools until years after the Republic had ceased to exist.[7]

---

2 C. W. Raines, Enduring Laws of the Republic of Texas, *Quarterly* II, 96; cites House Journal, 3rd. Cong. 169, 170.

3 Ibid., cites House Journal, Third Congress, p. 271.

4 Ibid., cites Laws of the Republic of Texas, 1st Sess. 3rd Cong p. 134.

5 Ibid, II, 96-100.

6 Eby, *Education*, 91.

7 Ibid., 92.

This failure to carry out the early plans does not mean that there was no educational work done; it simply means that the county officials did not take advantage of the opportunities offered to establish schools, and therefore that the education problem was left precisely where it had been—in the hands of religious groups, communities, or individual teachers. It is with the work of these groups, then, that the educational problem of the Republic is concerned.

These various agencies worked along individual lines. The religious groups established several schools before annexation. Rutersville College, probably the outstanding school of the Republic, was the work of the Methodists, and it was the greatest accomplishment of that organization.[8] The Baptists erected Baylor University at Independence in Washington County in 1841.[9] The Catholics, just then in the reorganization period, did not erect more than two parish schools.[10] The Presbyterians considered the erection of a college at their regular meeting of 1844, but nothing resulted before annexation.[11]

In addition to these schools under religious auspices, the more progressive settlements that thought seriously about educating their future citizens also did notable work in the field of education. These communities, few indeed, under the leadership of active and thoughtful citizens, erected some worthwhile school houses. Huntsville was a model town in this regard. Through voluntary contributions of the citizens, sufficient funds were raised for the erection of a building. The founder of the town, Pleasant Gray, donated the land, and in 1842, when Huntsville was scarcely six years old, it could boast of a substantial school building of brick, known as the "Brick Academy."[12] Nacogdoches, San

8 *Telegraph and Texas Register*, Jan. 20, 1841.

9 John Brown, *History of Texas*, (St. Louis, 1893) 2 vols., II, 510.

10 Sister Mary Angela Fitzmorris, *Four Decades of Catholicism in Texas, 1820-1860* (Washington, D. C. 1926), 67.

11 Robert Miller, Early Presbyterianism in Texas, *Quarterly*, XIX, 171.

12 Harry F. Estill, The Old Town of Huntsville, *Quarterly* III, 265.

Augustine and Marshall were other communities that sponsored schools. Each of these gave the name of University to its school.[13] The town of Liberty had a school as early as 1838 and advertised for a teacher in the following way:

> Agreeably to a resolution passed by the board of trustees of the town of Liberty notice is hereby given that a building has lately been erected in said town for the purpose of establishing an Academy capable of accommodating from forty to fifty pupils, for which a preceptor is wanted.
>
> Individuals wishing to make application for the above situation, must produce testimonials as to their sobriety, and attention to business to the Mayor W. W. Tenley, and be present to undergo an examination on the 15th day of May next.
>
> Geo. W. Miles, Sec.[14]

There really was never a shortage of teachers, the above instance being a rare example, since many itinerant teachers of adventurous disposition, and other individuals expecting to find an easy livelihood in the teaching profession, opened schools in the growing communities. Usually the people welcomed these enterprises because it gave them an opportunity to send their children to school in the home town. Many letters from teachers of this type are found in the Lamar correspondence. R. M. Chapman wrote from Pittsfield, Massachusetts, in 1838 that he proposed to establish a school in the Republic should there be an even chance of making a success of the enterprise.[15] Mr. Hamilton of Mobile, Alabama had similar ideas:

13 Eby, *Education*, 94.
14 *Telegraph and Texas Register*, April 28, 1838.
15 R. M. Chapman to Lamar, Jan. 1, 1838, *Lamar Papers* II, 13.

I have frequently entertained the idea of attempting to establish in Texas a literary insti-
tution, or college could suitable encouragement
be secured...The beginning must be made
therefore by establishing a preparatory or
grammar school—in which to train young
men for the regular college classes...It would
be highly gratifying to me could you favor me
with your opinion.[16]

These individual projects often materialized. Guadalupe
Academy, McKenzie Institute, Matagorda Academy and
Independence Academy were all private ventures.[17] The
Matagorda Academy advertised that first lessons in spell-
ing, reading and writing could be had for three dollars a
month; arithmetic, grammar, geography, history and composition were taught at six dollars a month. "For all the
higher branches of Science and Literature, and especially
the Mathematics and Latin and Greek languages" the
charges were nine dollars per month. This institute conducted classes from October 1 to July 1.[18]

It would almost seem from this enumeration of schools
and courses that education in Texas was fairly well organized. Such was not the case; education really was in a bad
way. The above enumeration just about exhausts the list,
and therefore the vast majority of communities was without
adequate school facilities. Little was done about the matter
and the result was a thoroughly disorganized state of affairs
that varied with each different community and got worse in
the more sparsely settled districts. Only haphazard efforts
were made to remedy a bad situation and the results were
not in the least uniform, all of which makes it hopelessly
impossible to classify the educational projects of that day.

----

16 Hamilton to Lamar, Nov. 21, 1838, *Lamar Papers*, II, 297.

17 Eby, *Education*, 94.

18 *Telegraph and Texas Register*, Spring 1841.

In general it may be said that primitiveness, simplicity, and crudeness were the characteristics of the early school houses. Square or rectangular structures built of logs were quite the accepted thing. A picture of the buildings that were somewhat common around 1838 is given by Mrs. Harris:

> The school house was built of rough planks and consisted of two rooms. The boys' room was without a plank floor, and there was no shutter to the door, nor glass to the window. Rough planks placed on barrels and nail kegs served for desks and chairs.[19]

Mr. Sparks attended a school of this type in the neighborhood of Nacogdoches. The building was of pine logs and covered a space fourteen by fourteen feet; it did not have a floor. The total enrollment of the school was eight.[20] James N. Smith, a Tennessee teacher, opened a school in Gonzales county in 1840. He charged $2.00 a month for tuition. It was the first school building in the neighborhood and "the neighbors soon cut logs and built a comfortable school house."[21] In many settlements even such crude buildings did not exist, and then classes were conducted out in the open air under the shade of a tree.[22]

Often classes were held in the homes of pioneers. The Kenny home was one of these. Miss McHenry, assisted by the lady of the house, Mrs. Kenny, was the teacher. This school opened in 1837 with a class of about twenty boys and girls; reading was the principal subject taught. After two or three terms the experiment was abandoned since it was a financial failure.[23] Schools of this type did not have any uniformity in regard to the time of opening and closing the sessions. Each teacher taught as long as he could induce a

---

19 Reminiscences of Mrs. Dilue Harris, *Quarterly*, IV, 188.

20 Recollections of S. F. Sparks, *Quarterly*, XII, 61.

21 Autobiography of James N. Smith, 24, University of Texas, Austin.

22 Erath, Memoirs, *Quarterly* XXVI, 224.

23 M. M. Kenny, Recollections of Early Schools, *Quarterly*, I, 285.

sufficient number of pupils to attend. Since the children worked in the fields and on the ranches, classes were held only when work was slack.[24]

Nor were teachers always sure of their pay. Quite often they were expected to accept in payment for their services, such surplus produce as farmers happened to have. Noah Smithwick tells us that Captain Beach, teacher at Webber's Prairie was obliged to accept payment in corn, for which there was no sale nearer than Austin, so the teacher had to borrow a team and haul it to market.[25] Gillett wrote to his friend Dr. Ashbel Smith:

> I have opened an academy about 3 miles from Washington and I think my prospects flattering...As an inducement to open a school Mr. Franquhr boards me Gratis—he sends 5—My patrons nearly all raise Cotton—so my pay is very sure.[26]

One of the greatest hindrances to making intellectual progress in the schools, such as they were, was the scarcity of school books. Books of any and every description were used—pupils were usually forced to use such as had been brought by their parents from the old states, whether they were suitable or not.[27] Naturally, classwork was impossible with an arrangement of that kind. What could be expected when a teacher tried to conduct a class in reading and found out that one boy had Robinson Crusoe for his book, several others the Life of Washington, one an illustrated edition of Goldsmith's Natural History, and still others had no books at all?[28] Often such a situation could not be remedied since few books were offered for sale. Even well-equipped stores that carried school supplies, such as the general store

---

24 Eby, *Education*, 103.

25 Smithwick, *Evolution of a State*, 231.

26 Gillette to Smith, Sept. 17, 1841, MS. Ashbel Smith Papers.

27 Wallis. *Sixty Years on the Brazos*, 33.

28 Kenny, Early Schools, *Quarterly* I, 288.

in Harrisburg, were limited and usually carried only "Murray's Grammars, Walker's Dictionaries, slate pencils and lead pencils."[29]

Under these conditions, it is not surprising to find that people who were able, because of financial independence, to provide for the education of their children in other ways, did not hesitate to do so. The wealthy usually sent their children back to the States or employed tutors. Major Sutherland sent his daughter to school in Alabama.[30] In 1843 three of the Erskine children were sent to Virginia for their schooling.[31] Mary McNeil of San Antonio was sent to relatives in Mississippi where she attended school.[32] Moseley Baker's daughter, Fanny, received her education in Alabama, and the children of Mrs. A. C. Allen were also sent East to be educated.[33] Mirabeau Lamar, the President of Texas who advocated the establishment of an educational system, found it to his advantage to employ a tutor and have his daughter instructed at home.[34] And Adolphus Sterne employed a private tutor at six dollars a month for his two sons Charles and Joseph.[35]

Since the majority of the well-to-do educated their children privately or in the States,[36] they did not care about supporting the local schools. It is for this reason that the schools that did exist never flourished. Without the support of the wealthy, the obligation of maintaining schools fell on the poorer who were unable to do so, and under such an arrangement no first class school system could develop.

It can safely be asserted that the educational institutions of Texas did not have a great influence on the mental and

---

29 Looscan, Harris County, *Quarterly* XVIII, 202.

30 Sam Maverick to Mary A. Maverick, Dec. 29, 1838, MS. Maverick Papers.

31 The Diary and Letters of Michael Erskine, 24, University of Texas, Austin.

32 Maverick, Memoirs, 89.

33 Bower to Smith, July 11, 1844, MS. Ashbel Smith Papers.

34 Garret to Lamar, Oct. 2, 1838, *Lamar* Papers V, 199.

35 Sterne, Diary, *Quarterly* XXXV, 241.

36 Eby, *Education*, 93.

cultural development of the people. The moral training of
the citizens, as measured by their reaction toward religion,
was about as fruitless. This might be surprising in view of
the fact that the Mexican nation had tried to avoid just such
a thing, by providing in its colonization laws that all immigrants profess the Catholic faith. This stipulation, however,
was never rigidly enforced. Such as did fulfill this require-
ment did so in many cases because of the possible advantages
they might derive, rather than from religious conviction.
These were only nominal Catholics, and naturally they were
not influenced by the teachings of that religion.[37] John Linn,
one of the early colonists who had many contacts with
pioneers all over the state, when making reference to the
religious qualifications of the immigrants, says that not one
out of ten of the colonists introduced into Texas was
Catholic.[38]

In fact it could not have been otherwise, since the Catholic religion was almost nonexistent before 1840, there being
practically no priests in Texas before that time.[39] Father
Odin, later bishop of Texas, came to that country in 1840,
and an examination of his diary shows that religious rites
were poorly administered. The sick often died without the
consolations of religion, and confessions had not been heard
for fourteen years. Baptizing, burying the dead, and cele-
brating marriages were about the only functions of the
ministry, and for these exorbitant fees were charged.[40] A
further examination of the same diary shows that, not
counting the old missions that were in various states of ruin,
there were only three Catholic churches in Texas in 1840.[41] It
was due to the zealous Bishop Odin that Catholicism was
revived, and as early as 1846, ten churches and chapels had

---

37 Erath, Memoirs, *Quarterly* XXVI, 224.

38 Fitzmorris, *Catholicism*, 37, cites Linn, *Reminiscences*, 283.

39 Ibid., 40

40 Ibid., 37, cites Linn, *Reminiscences*, 50.

41 Fathers P. F Parisot and C. J. Smith (editors), *History of the Catholic Church in the Diocese of San Antonio*, (San Antonio, 1897), 63.

been erected and four others were in the process of construction.[42]

Bishop Odin was not the only one who took note of spiritual laxity. The Reverend Sneed, a Methodist minister on a visit to Texas, was impressed by "the great spiritual destitution of the people" and volunteered to enter the missionary field.[43] Oscar Addison, another Methodist minister, was not so optimistic when he wrote to his father and mother in 1843:

> I have now gone 3/4 of the way round my circuit and find nothing cheering or encouraging, many of the members have backslidden, and are spiritually dead—some have been going to dancing school, and some have joined the Baptists![44]

A Houston paper in 1839 complains that Houston had a theater, a court house, a jail and even a capitol, but not a single church.[45] And the citizens of San Felipe, the original headquarters of the Anglo-Americans, were likewise without a church.[46]

However, there were some churches erected during the years the Republic existed. The Catholics, as has already been stated, put up several. The city of Houston had a Protestant Episcopal church by 1840.[47] The Methodists, very active during the Republic, took steps to erect a church as early as 1837. One of their missionaries wrote in his journal: "Oct. 19th [1837] we reached San Augustine and preached four nights in succession. There I began a subscription for building a church. In less than two weeks a lot was deeded, $3500 were subscribed, trustees were appointed...The same

42 Fitzmorris, op. cit., 67; cites *Metropolitan Catholic Almanac.*

43 O. M. Addison, Life and Times of Joseph D. Sneed, MS. Addison Papers.

44 O. M. Addison to Father and Mother, Feb. 12, 1843, MS. Addison Papers.

45 *Morning Star*, (Houston) April 18, 1839, Oct. 8, 1839; June 18, 1839.

46 Rosa Kleberg, Some of My Early Experiences in Texas, *Quarterly* I, 300.

47 Brown, *Texas*, II, 516.

missionary under the date of January 17, 1838, continues: "Today the corner stone of a Methodist Episcopal Church was laid..."[48] Ministers of other religions were likewise industrious, and had organized churches before annexation.

These church buildings were the exception rather than the rule, and missionaries making their rounds often had to conduct services in private homes.[49] When a missionary happened along, any kind of building available was used. Adolphus Sterne records in his diary: "Sunday the 27th [1843]...the Religious People all assembled in the Court House to hear Parson Rhodes preach..."[50] But the most common practice was to hold camp meetings and revival meetings out in the open. This really was the kind of religious influence that reached the greatest number of Texans. The early ministers of the gospel were missionaries in the real sense of the word—a good deal of their time was taken up in traveling. The sad state of affairs in the Catholic church impelled Fathers Timon and Lelebaria to spend a considerable time in touring the country in 1839 from Galveston as far west as San Antonio, in an effort to revive religion.[51] The same motives impelled Father Odin in 1840, and he spent three months in and about San Antonio trying to bring Catholics back into the fold and to add new members to the church.[52] Ministers of other religions likewise did much traveling. In the earlier times there were no definite fields assigned to these men and they labored wherever a providential opening was found.[53] The Reverend Addison's diary gives us an idea of the extent of travel:

Tuesday Jan. 1st 1839, rode 25 miles to Mr. Wormleys. Wednesday 2, rode 31 miles to Brother Voss'es.

---

48 Dora Fowler Arthur, Jottings From the Old Journal of Littleton Fowler, *Quarterly* II, 78.
49 Smithwick, *Evolution of a State*, 231
50 Sterne, Diary, *Quarterly* XXXVI, 217.
51 Fitzmorris, *Catholicism*, 44-46.
52 Parisot and Smith, *Catholic Church in San Antonio Diocese*, 59.
53 Thrall, *Methodism*, 53.

Thursday 3, rode 36 miles to Mr. Monticues,
   Paid 1.00 cts.
Friday 4, rode 33 miles (paid 25 cts. Ferriage)
   to Mr. Adams'es, paid 1.00 cts.
Saturday 5, rode 53 miles to Brother Loyds.
Sunday 6, preached from Mat vii-7, rode 7
   miles.
Monday 7, rode 16 miles to Holly Springs to
   Brother Epps'es.
Tuesday 8, rode 30 miles to Oxford, Staid
   with Brother Jennings.[54]

These trips were by no means easy to make. Indians
frequented the wilds between the settlements and proved a
constant danger. Often ministers while traveling alone
would be heavily armed.[55] When Father Odin made his first
trip to San Antonio in 1840 he made the journey with an
armed wagon train to protect himself against attacks from
the Indians.[56]

Some idea of the character of the camp meetings these
traveling missionaries conducted can be gathered from their
diaries and journals. Jesse Hord, a Methodist minister, in his
diary under date of January 31, 1839, thus describes a revival meeting:

The scene was novel, solemn, imposing. A
cloth tent, quite a log-heap on fire, surrounded
by men and women anxiously inquiring the
"way of life," and that in the midst of the
almost undisturbed jungle of Old Caney bottom. My impressioned spirit caught the inspi-
ration of the scene. I read to them the word of
God, sung, prayed, exhorted them "to flee the
wrath to come," and invited mourners, though

54 O. M. Addison Journal, MS. Addison Papers.
55 From an early picture of the Rev. A. J. Potter, Methodist Minister; original in Westmoor-
land College, San Antonio.
56 Parisot and Smith, *Catholic Church in San Antonio Diocese*, 59.

we had no "mourners' bench" nor altar. I entreated them to fall on their knees upon God's green earth, where they were, and in the name of the Lord Jesus Christ implore the mercy of God in the forgiveness of their sins. Many if not every sinner of the assembled company, bowed and cried aloud for mercy. This service continued to a late hour of the night unabated in interest. Several professed to have obtained a degree of comfort. There was, however one poor soul who from the beginning seemed to be overwhelmed with a sense of the guilt and burden of sin, whose conversion was clear, pentecostal. The tongue of fire seemed to rest upon her, and she confessed her conversion in the language of praise and thanksgiving to God. This lady, Mrs. Tone, with other persons, joined the Church at the close of our service for the night.[57]

These revivals were not daily affairs—there were not enough ministers in the land for that—and the territory to be covered was so large that frequently the people would not come under the influence of a minister for months. Efforts were made to remedy this situation and to systematize the holding of revivals. Instructions to ministers in 1839 were: "Each of you will follow the other and make a round each 6 weeks. You will have a Quarterly meeting in each Circuit . . . where and when you judge will be for the best."[58]

The diary of Reverend Hord indicates that the people were often waiting for the periodical visit of ministers.

January 8, [1839]—This day I traveled thirty miles up Old Caney to a settlement. The people

---

57 Thrall, *Methodism*, 62.
58 Fowler to Rev. Sneed, July 16, 1839, MS. Addison Papers.

had heard that a preacher was coming, and they were much elated, so much so that when I got to the settlement I was thus hailed as I passed: I suspect you are the man of whom we have heard. Won't you preach for us tomorrow? Certainly these people were hungry.

January 9.—Today I had the exquisite pleasure of preaching to this people, so hungry for the gospel. They literally drank in the word, all suffused in tears. "O my soul, praise the Lord!" "Glory be to God!" After services I traveled some fourteen miles to a Mrs. Hardemanus, where I had a good rest.[59]

Quite naturally some people objected to this sort of missionary work, and did not approve of the missionary's efforts nor of the reaction of the people to his promptings. Ashbel Smith, a Houston citizen, was not so favorably impressed by these proceedings, and after witnessing them for a week, wrote to his friend in New York:

Methodists of this town Houston are in a state of horrible—of frightful excitement—which has lasted already eight or ten days and attracts crowds of spectators. No pen or tongue could give you an adequate description of those riotous scenes—a person must see & hear in order to be convinced of their mad extravagancies & I fancy most will distrust the evidence of their senses. They call it a revival.[60]

A similar impression was made on Adolphus Sterne of Nacogdoches:

A Mr. Rhodes preached, that is to say, he made a noise, rather productive of scaring babys

---

59 Thrall, *Methodism*, 59.
60 Bower to Smith, Sept 3, 1845, MS. Ashbel Smith Papers.

than to convert men to Christianity, when a man undertakes to teach others that which he does not understand himself he must make it up in Bawling, or ranting, or talking, right down nonsense.[61]

One might believe that such reflections came only from chronic complainers or from persons who were prejudiced one way or the other. But such descriptions could not be applied to either Smith or Sterne. The former is known for his moderate views, and the latter's writings indicate that he was an impartial observer. He was favorably impressed when witnessing another religious ceremony, one that was conducted with propriety and decorum, and wrote concerning it:

> Sunday 31 Jan. 1841...was introduced to the reverend Mr. Timan and the rt revd. Mr. Odin, the first Vicar general of the Pope in Texas, the second the Bishop (that will be of Texas) two most learned men, they said Mass at the Stone House this morning, and notwithstanding the bad weather there was the largest, and most respectable congregation present that I have ever seen, during the performance of the Service, Mr. Timan preached...in such Chaste and eloquent language as perhaps never has been used by any Divine in Nacogdoches before.[62]

Under the religious conditions as they existed in the Republic of Texas a great deal of moral training was almost impossible. The fervor that was often aroused by the fiery admonitions of the ministers of the gospel lasted but a short while, as the preacher could not consolidate his work, and the people, left to themselves, soon forgot the good advice they had received.

---

61 Sterne, Diary, *Quarterly*, XXXIV, 264
62 Ibid., XXXI, 185.

This absence of a thorough moral training was often magni-
fied, and conditions attendant upon such a state were so
distorted and enlarged, that it was soon the common opinion of many people living in various parts of the United
States that Texas was a country filled with outlaws and
banditti of every description. Much has been written about
these Texas Bad Men and their utter disregard for law and
order; some of it is true, much half-true, and a great deal of
it is utterly false. When reading about the influence of law
and the legal system on the average Texan, one is con-
fronted with a great many conflicting reports. Some point
out that certain sections of the country were made less
attractive because of the "thieves and mean wretches" who
inhabited them.[63] Or they thoroughly agree with the opinion
Francis Sheridan expressed when he wrote to a friend in
England:

> Murder and every other Crime is of great
> frequency in Texas and the Perpetrators es-
> cape with the greatest impunity ... It is consid-
> ered unsafe to walk through the Streets of the
> principal Towns without being armed. The
> Bowie Knife is the weapon most in vogue.[64]

Others insist "that there are few countries, either old or
new, where good order is so well appreciated, and the laws
so generally respected and maintained by the force of public
opinion."[65] Before Mrs. Houstoun visited Texas she had
heard a good many things about the people, and after she
left it she thus recorded her impressions.

> If we are to believe many of the writers of today,
> murders are to be met at every town, life is not
> safe...private property is never respected...
> These accusations are almost entirely false

63 Maverick to Adams, Sept. 8, 1839, MS. Maverick Papers.
64 Sheridan to Garraway, July 12, 1840, British Correspondence, *Quarterly* XV, 221.
65 Ikin, *Texas*, 74.

...a glance at the general character of the people, one must feel that they are undeserved.
The rarity of the criminal acts is rendered
remarkable by the almost non-existence of
courts of law...[66]

It is highly probable that all the writers of these reports
were right—as each wrote from his own point of view.
Those who expected to find the people exhibit the virtues of
convent life were certainly disappointed, and they did not
hesitate to state their opinions, usually with a bitterness in
proportion to their disappointment. The others expecting to
find a hard-drinking, jovial band of pioneers, men and
women to whom the worst had already happened, were
likewise forced to change their opinion; they concluded the
Texans were quite a law-abiding set of people after all.

An examination of the files of the newspapers in the
Republic throws some light on the Texan's attitude toward
law. The *Telegraph and Texas Register* carried, on June 24,
1837, this item:

The lives of our citizens are frequently endan-
gered by the careless use of fire arms which
are hourly discharged in the precincts of the
city.[67]

A few months later the same paper gives an account of
the murder of Mr. Kelcy by a man named Hubbard. The
writer of the article said that this was the first case in Houston in which someone had "fallen a victim to the disgraceful
custom of wearing deadly weapons."[68] And about a half
year later we find the following:

Duelling. We rejoice to state that although
no less than a dozen challenges have been

66 Houston, *Texas and the Gulf of Mexico*, (Philadelphia, 1845), 187.
67 *Telegraph and Texas Register*, June 24, 1837.
68 Ibid., Sept. 23, 1837.

presented and accepted by various individuals in this city, [Houston] within the last three months, not a single duel has taken place.[69]

This good record evidently was kept up for some months, and the editor devoted an editorial to congratulating his fellow citizens on this record:

> It must be a matter of sincere pleasure to every philanthropist, that, not a single duel has occurred in this portion of Texas for many months.[70]

Not only was progress made in lessening the number of duels, but it seems that conduct in general was on the upgrade—maybe the ministers were busy at that time—for we read in the same paper under a still later date: "We are glad to find that our citizens are gradually relinquishing the practice of wearing weapons..."[71]

Some time after this the editor suddenly got indignant about the conduct of the citizens and complained about the large number of murders perpetrated or attempted.

> Almost every mail that has reached us for the last few weeks, has brought accounts of some petty rencounter or bloody brawl, that has resulted in the death or wounding of some individual...We shall rejoice when our unhappy republic shall cease to be the arena of private feuds and disgraceful brawls, that tend alike to degrade those who engage in them, and to fasten opprobrium upon the national character.[72]

---

69 *Telegraph and Texas Register*, Feb. 24, 1838
70 Ibid., April 21, 1838.
71 Ibid., May 5, 1838.
72 Ibid., Jan. 19, 1842.

Those inclined to lawlessness were certainly not deterred by the possibility of having their offence brought before an efficient jury, and having a competent judge pronounce sentence, after a thorough analysis of the case.[73] Courts of this type were extremely rare, if they existed at all. A fair idea of the lack of dignity and decorum that usually was witnessed in a court room may be gathered from this description of a court setting:

> There was a very gentlemanly man as Judge—Morriss. The District Attorney as prosecution for the Republic [was] opposed by half dozen lawyers—ready of speech and loads of references—from Magna Charter upwards—The Court was over a crockery store used on Sunday for a Methodist Chapel—the Judge [was] chewing his qued—thrown back in his chair—his legs thrown up on his desk—the District Attorney [was] chewing and smoking.

> The Counsel for the Prisoner D° D° & [there was] a small quantity of whittling...I saw the weed in the mouth of some of the lookers on—order was kept in the Court—but ever and anon [there was] a squirt of Tobacco juice on the floor...[74]

However even courts of this kind were capable of dispensing speedy justice—and of doing so without much formality. This point is well illustrated by reading several entries in the diary of J. H. Herndon, a Kentucky citizen who made a trip through Texas in 1837-38. Herndon was particularly interested in a case that was before the Houston Bar, and wrote the highlights of the case in his diary. A faithful reproduction of the diary tells the story:

73 cf. Bollaert's analysis of 3 cases submitted to the courts. Manuscript, 190-192.
74 Bollaert, Manuscript, 191.

March 22/1838 Fine day—4 criminals whipd
[sic] at the post—Jones convicted of murder. A
plainer case than which has seldom been submitted to a jury.

March 23/1838 Quick convicted of Murder— a
case similar to Jones's—Killed Mandord Wood,
a Bro of Ferdinando and Benj. Wood N. Y.—
Quick a savage bloodthirsty, malicious looking devil. Grand Jury dischgd. After having
presented 270 Inditments [sic]. 4 for Murder 4
treason 8 arson 40 Larceny—The Bar gave a
supper to the Grand jury—high meeting,
some gloriously drunk—

March 24/38 Judge Robertson sentenced John
Quick and James Jones to be hung on Wednes-
day next between the hours of 10 8 2 P. M.—
An excellent sentence—

March 25/38—All peacable—a decided reform
in the morals of Houston.

25th Jones the convict attempted to kill himself by shooting but shot over his head.

28th A delightful day, worthy of other
deeds—140 men order'd out to guard the
Criminals to the gallows—a concourse of from
2000 to 3000 persons on the ground and among
the whole not a single sympathetic tear was
dropped—Quick addressed the crowd in a
stern composed & hardened manner entirely
unmoved up to the moment of swinging off the
cart—Jones seemed frightened altho' as hardened in crime as Quick—They swung off at 2
o'clock P. M. and were cut down in 35 minutes
not having made the slightest struggle. [75]

---

75 T. H. Herndon. Diary.

This probably was a most unusual occurrence since we see it given great prominence in the Houston *Telegraph*. The editor of that paper makes a three column story out of the affair, but does not really add anything to Herndon's account.[76]

Sensational happenings of this character evidently did much to instill fear into the people and prompt them to conduct themselves in such a way as to avoid all involving contacts with the courts. Still, to repeat, it was not the judicial system that influenced the citizens and made them law abiding. The most powerful influence on right conduct was probably the justice that was meted out by groups of citizens who were interested in preserving order, and who were not remiss about using their own methods of ridding the neighborhood of all undesirables.[77]

---

76 *Telegraph and Texas Register*, March 31. 1838.
77 Houstoun, *Texas*, 187; Wallis, *Sixty Years on the Brazos*, 92.

Mudholes, Redbacks & Scalps:
Economic & Social Problems

The Camino Real, or King's Highway, is one of the famous roads in the Southwest; it traversed the entire Republic of Texas. Starting at the Rio Grande, it passed through San Antonio, Bastrop, Nacogdoches and extended beyond the Sabine River. To the south and east of the King's Highway, often called the Old San Antonio Road, several other roads, or more accurately, trails, crossed the wilds and connected with either the King's Highway, or with each other. In addition to this there were other roads of local importance, that amounted to nothing more than trackless courses through the wilderness or prairies. The condition of the roads often made traveling uncomfortable, sometimes hazardous, and occasionally impossible. Roads in the modern sense did not exist at all; those that are referred to were little more than well-beaten paths, serviceable only in dry weather.

With such a limited number of roads, travel and communication were rendered exceedingly difficult, and travelers frequently had to be content with striking out in the general direction of their destination. It was not unusual to be obliged to depend on a compass. The Reverend McCalla, while traveling near Bastrop was given directions and he then "rode five miles, guided by the compass, and fell into a promised road."[1]

But finding one's way was not always so simple and the traveler frequently got lost. Bollaert while traveling with his companions from San Antonio to Columbus got off the trail and was soon lost. After a vain effort to regain his route, he decided to make the best of his hard luck and camp for the night. At about that time assistance came; but let Bollaert finish the story:

> When we heard the distant bark of a dog, [we] concluded we could not be very far from

---

1 McCalla, *Texas*, 28.

a settlement. We hollowed 'like mad' for half an hour when we were responded to by human voices. Three gentlemen from a plantation about 1/4 mile off kindly came to our assistance...taking us to their habitation.[2]

"A man in Spectacles from Houston" gave Adolphus Sterne directions for traveling, but it was not long before Sterne got off the trail, and his effort to straighten things out by a short cut through the woods only complicated the situation still more, so that in the evening, after a day's traveling, he found himself ten miles from the place he had left in the morning.[3] Even Sam Maverick, a seasoned traveler, lost his way in the neighborhood of Victoria.[4]

For the average traveler the usual method of getting from place to place was on horseback. For example, Ashbel Smith tells of a journey he took to the city of Austin in this way.[5] Routine business trips to the towns, such as getting the mail, were frequently on horseback.[6] In fact the practice was so common that even ladies adopted it as the most practical way of getting from place to place;[7] it is known that the daughters of Sam and Mary Maverick traveled in this way.[8]

The vehicles that did exist were of the crudest type. Ox-carts were the most common for all heavy hauling; immigrants finding it necessary to move their household goods frequently hired conveyances of this kind.[9] For lighter travel, buggies were used, but usually only by the well-to-do.[10] Mr. Holland remembers that the city of Austin,

---

2 Bollaert, Manuscript, II, 137.

3 Sterne, Diary, *Quarterly*, XXXI, 81.

4 Sam to Mary Maverick, Dec. 29, 1838, MS. Maverick Papers.

5 Smith to Barnard, Dec. 5, 1839, MS. Ashbel Smith Papers.

6 Wallis, *Sixty Years on the Brazos*, 90. 91.

7 Lubbock, *Six Decades in Texas*, 57.

8 Mary A. Maverick, MS. Diary, 29.

9 Wallis, op. cit., 10-11.

10 Lubbock, op. cit., 77.

in the forties, did not have buggies; the only sort of conveyance was a "rickety stage coach" that had a very irregular schedule.[11] An editorial in a Houston paper as late as 1841, gives some particulars about stage coaches and some information on transportation in general:

> Stages—We are pleased to learn that Messrs. Smith and Jones, mail contractors for the route from this place to Austin, have made arrangements to keep up the communication by means of carriages. These vehicles will commence running this week, and will doubtless continue throughout the year. This cannot but be gratifying to every man who desires to see improved, all means of communication between Houston and the upper country. The running of carriages for the conveyance of passengers, will remedy in a great measure, the delay, vexation and expense which have heretofore been incident to a trip to Austin. It has been necessary for a stranger on reaching Houston, to spend a day or two in purchasing a horse and equipments, and in making other preparations for a tedious ride of 170 miles on horse back, in order to reach the seat of government. We wish the most complete success to these enterprising gentlemen.[12]

With an actual scarcity of highways, and with existing roads in constant need of repair, it is not surprising to learn that the traveler made poor progress. A gentleman setting out for California across the Republic of Texas wrote when nearing Austin: "I suppose you think we ought to be half way to California before this, but we have moved along very slowly, partly from choice and partly on account of bad

---

11 J. K. Holland, Reminiscences of Austin and Old Washington, *Quarterly*, I, 92.
12 *Telegraph and Texas Register*, April 21, 1841.

roads."[13] During the evacuation following the Mexican invasion into San Antonio in the early part of 1842, despite all efforts to reach the eastern part of Texas without the least possible delay, the people traveled only five miles the first day, twenty-two the second, twelve the third and twelve the fourth; and they were going over a highway.[14]

Probably the greatest impediment to travel was the lack of bridges. Very few existed, and they were frequently toll bridges.[15] Dangerous streams were crossed by means of ferries, and even then much was wanting. The approaches were neglected and never kept in a state of repair, so that accidents were frequent. To get up and down the steep banks leading to the ferry was as difficult "as to ascend the roof of a house or precipice," and teams and oxen in attempting to negotiate the difficult maneuver were sometimes precipitated into the river.[16] Less difficult streams were crossed by swimming the horses over, and towing the baggage across on a raft of logs.[17]

The only really good avenues of transportation lay along the sandy beaches of the Gulf. Mrs. Holley traveled along a section and described it as "nearly 30 miles long, & as hard & smooth as a floor...such a road can be traveled by night as by day. It is delightful by moonlight."[18] But the beach never was a great highway of commerce. The flow of traffic was into the interior and not along the coast, and when there was coastwise traffic it was carried on by means of boats.

Roads that were poor when they were in their best shape were practically impassable in wet weather. It was not unusual for a traveler in stage coaches to be obliged to work his way "by carrying a fence rail on his shoulder for long

13 Journal of Lewis B. Harris, 1836-1842, *Quarterly*, XXV, 195.
14 Maverick, Diary, 1.
15 Sterne, Diary, *Quarterly*, XXX, 319.
16 *Telegraph and Texas Register*, Jan. 27, 1841.
17 Sterne, Diary, *Quarterly*, XXXI, 81.
18 Holley to Brand, Nov. 27, 1840, MS. Holley Letters.

distances and helping to pry the vehicle out of mudholes, in order to reach his destination at all."[19] Sam Maverick wrote to Mrs. Maverick that the roads between the Colorado and Brazos rivers were in terrible shape due to the recent rains, saying: "I was obliged in the worst places to relieve the mule by getting off and leading for a mile at a time."[20] Doctor Lockhart never forgot the journey he made from Houston to Washington in 1840. He hired several ox-wagons to move his possessions and make the trip.

> After loading them up [Lockhart wrote] we started sometime in February for our destination. The roads were in their worst condition. If we traveled five miles a day we did well...After passing through much mud, water and other trials and troubles, we finally reached the town of Washington.[21]

When the roads were in their worst condition traffic usually stopped completely. Mrs. Holley, living at Peach Point in 1838, was anxiously awaiting the arrival of her brother Henry, so that she could transact some important business. While waiting she thus explained the delay to her daughters:

> He has no doubt been detained on his route. It has been impossible to travel much — a terrible inconvenience — so many people have to go over the country at this time...I am only afraid of delay caused by bad weather which stops all business...[22]

The irregular departure of the mail during a wet season was explained in an editorial of the Houston *Telegraph*:

---

19 Holland, Reminiscences, *Quarterly*, I, 92.
20 Sam to Mary A. Maverick, Dec. 29, 18.18, MS. Maverick Papers.
21 Wallis, *Sixty Years on the Brazos*, 10-11.
22 Mrs. Holley to Henrietta, Feb. 8, 1838, MS. Holley Letters.

> To our Subscribers—The late unusually wet weather has rendered the roads all over the country so bad, that the contractors on the few mail routes still kept up by the post office department, have been compelled to suspend operations; hence the disappointment of our distant subscribers. Three different numbers of this paper are now lying in the post office here, awaiting the regular departure of the mails over their several routes...[23]

The officials of the Republic did not do much to remedy a bad situation, and while it is easy to find references to new roads being opened, it is much rarer to read that the existing ones were repaired. Sterne did not approve of this procedure and noted it in his diary:

> Jan. 11, 1841...Road Commissioners met, more new Roads were Ordered to be Surveyed — bad business if the Public Roads we now have would be kept in good order we would do much better then [sic] to make new bad Roads...[24]

Those that existed were often "wide and handsome," and had they been taken care of, would have been very serviceable.[25] But such was their customary state of disrepair that, even on the principal streets of Houston, it was quite usual to see ox-wagons bogged in chuckholes long after a rain.[26] Hollows and ditches which were a hazard to traffic became no less a menace to health by retaining pools of stagnating water for weeks at a time.[27]

---

23 *Telegraph and Texas Register*, Jan. 20, 1841.

24 Sterne, Diary, *Quarterly* XXXI, 182.

25 Holley to Brand, Nov. 12, 1842, MS. Holley Letters.

26 Wallis, *Sixty Years on the Brazos*, 10.

27 Winkler, Seat of Government, *Quarterly* X, 187, cites the *Telegraph and Texas Register*, Oct. 11, 1837.

Since lines of communication were open only during fair weather, produce moved along regular lines only when circumstances were favorable, and when unexpected rains were encountered in the course of a journey which "transformed the black soil into vast beds of wax, they [farmers] were sometimes several weeks on the trip."[28] More frequently, however, the rainy season was foreseen, and at such times flat-boats would convey the cotton and other produce down the small rivers and on to the shipping or distributing centers.[29]

In fact the smaller streams were regularly used by those living along the banks to transport the heavier commodities to market.[30] The possibility of using the rivers as regular avenues of commerce was frequently discussed, and at times steamers made trips far into the interior to demonstrate the practicability of navigation.[31] Still no regular service was established probably because the level of the rivers was too inconstant; besides, boats had to be of light draught, and this prevented them from taking on cargoes sufficiently large to make the trip profitable.

The only river traffic that did develop was a commercial venture between Houston and Galveston. Already in 1838 Houston boasted of four steam boats that made regular trips to Galveston,[32] and after 1840 "regular mail packets began running between Houston and Galveston."[33]

The transportation system of Texas certainly did not contribute anything toward establishing thriving commercial centers in the Republic. Neither did its financial system. The first years following the war for independence were trying ones. Establishing a new government, and putting it on a sound financial basis is always a difficult task; the

---

28 Smithwick, *Evolution of a State,* 264.

29 Bollaert, Manuscript, II, 142.

30 Newton and Gambrell, *Texas,* 123.

31 Houstoun, *Texas,* 184.

32 Bollaert, Manuscript, 12.

33 Looscan, Harris County, *Quarterly,* XIX, 49.

financial problem that faced the first Texas legislature was rendered more difficult, since it was coincident with the general hard times in the United States following the Panic of 1837. Aid from the United States was therefore almost entirely out of the question, and aid from its other neighbor, Mexico, was of course unthinkable. The new legislators set about solving the problem with the confidence of youth, and committed the blunder of issuing large quantities of paper money, backed only by government lands that had practically no market value. The system ran the inevitable course of all such systems, and additional issues of money further depreciated the circulating medium. By 1839, two years after paper money was first issued, currency had depreciated to about twenty-two cents on the dollar,[34] and in 1842, when the government refused to accept paper money in payment for taxes and other public dues, its value fell so low that it became practically worthless. An early history of Texas thus sums up the financial situation:

> During the Republic, and particularly in the latter days thereof, people became apparently very poor in the circulating medium. All kinds of property were very much depreciated, and stockcattle had no convertible cash values; business transactions became very limited between citizens, and nearly all their trade was carried on in barter, the exchange of commodities; and in the sales of property and effects, on credit, to be paid for, at some future time, in other property.[35]

Those who came to Texas in 1836 and 1837, did not at that time have a devaluated currency to contend with, but perhaps their condition was even worse because, outside of foreign coins, there was practically no circulating medium.

_____

34 Waller to Lamar, July 11, 1839, *Lamar Papers*, III, 40.
35 D. E. Braman, *Braman's Information about Texas*, (Philadelphia:1857), 80.

The writings of two German immigrants who came to the country at this time illustrate the shortage of currency. Rosa Kleberg, who had brought some fine linen tablecloths along, was forced to trade them for various necessary provisions.[36] George Erath purchased livestock by exchanging things he brought along, particularly his expensive clothes. After he had built up quite a livestock industry he did all his trading with cattle, and when his daughter edited his memoirs she commented on this practice by saying:

> To a certain extent a cow and a calf had come to be used as legal tender for ten dollars. If a man wished to say he had paid fifty dollars for a yoke of steers, very likely he said, even if he had paid in money, that he gave five cows and calves for them. The observation that cows and calves were ten dollar bills and hogs and chickens silver change was common.[37]

When currency became greatly devaluated, conditions of course were just as bad as if no money had existed, and barter again became the chief method of trading. As good money was very scarce those who possessed it were usually able to buy more cheaply.[38] A good illustration of this fact is found in Mrs. Holley's letter to her sister. Mrs. Holley moved to Galveston in 1842, and was asked to pay two dollars to the drayman for bringing her baggage to her new quarters. However, when the transferman found out that he was to be paid in silver, he demanded only twenty-five cents.[39] The curate in San Antonio, due to the scarcity of money, was obliged to accept produce in return for his services, and when he got things he could not use, he set out to barter for the things he required.[40]

---

36 Rosa Kleberg, Early Experiences, *Quarterly* II, 170.
37 Erath, Memoirs, *Quarterly* XXVI, 225.
38 Bollaert, Manuscript, II, 143.
39 Holley to Brand, Nov. 12, 1842, MS. Holley Letters.
40 Bollaert, Manuscript, II, 108.

Paging through the diary of Adolphus Sterne we find many references to the shortage of money. On September 5, 1842, Sterne wrote: "Nelson paid me a Cow worth twelve dollars on account of his Boarding."[41] The following week he again wrote: "Mr. Nelson paid One Barrel of flour for his board for one month."[42] And on December 12, 1843 Sterne wrote in his diary: "let Mr. Dwyer have 16 yards of Towels at 30 cents per yard, to be paid in waggoning."[43] The Nacogdoches merchant was not the only one to do business in this fashion. The *Northern Standard*, the influential Clarksville newspaper, carried a series of advertisements listing the articles which would be received in lieu of money as subscription for the paper. They included beeswax, honey, lard, tallow, brick, plank, rails, wheat and wheat flour.[44] Even Mirabeau B. Lamar was short of cash and exchanged 500 acres of land near Copano for a horse.[45] This system of bartering and trading impressed an English visitor as being so primitive that he thought a trader's books with its entries: "Cotton for Sugar & Coffee—Bacon for Boots—Corn for Calomel & Quinine & Whiskey—Beef for Brandy" would be an interesting manuscript to present to the British Museum.[46]

If the primitiveness of the transportation system, and the elementary character of the exchange proceedings did not constantly remind the inhabitants that they were in a pioneering land, then the frequent Indian troubles certainly did. The Indians were a constant source of trouble throughout the time of the Republic and for many years thereafter; neither President Lamar's aggressive and hostile attitude nor President Houston's conciliatory and persuasive methods settled the question. The Western and less thickly settled

---

41 Sterne, Diary, *Quarterly* XXXIV, 161.
42 Ibid., XXXIV, 164.
43 Ibid., XXXVI, 315.
44 *Northern Standard*, Aug. 20, 1842-Dec. 23, 1842; Sept. 3, 1842.
45 Lamar to Griffith, Aug. 15, 1838, *Lamar Papers*, II, 202.
46 Bollaert, Manuscript, II, 9.

districts were particularly subject to Indian depredations, and diaries, newspapers and memoirs are filled with allusions to their outrages.

One of the early white citizens of San Antonio tells of the Indians' method of attack:

> The Indians were always lurking around in small bodies hiding close to town, waiting for an opportunity to strike without danger to themselves. We were compelled to learn this through many murders and robberies. They would suddenly appear from the river bottom, from behind a clump of trees, from a gully, and sometimes from the tall grass. It seemed they were always on the watch everywhere, but only acted at the most favorable moments.[47]

Sneaking about frontier towns in this fashion the Indians often disturbed the citizens,[48] and frequently delayed travelers in setting out on proposed trips until several going in the same direction could form a company large enough to awe the Red Man and prevent him from attacking.[49]

The Indians frequently went on the warpath to obtain horses and food supplies. Moreover they were often urged on by the Mexicans who would not accept the Texas war for independence as final and who still had hopes of accomplishing something by harassing the people in this fashion.[50] But regardless of what prompted the uprisings, death usually resulted from them.

The private secretary of President Houston concluded an official letter from Austin on February 23, 1843, with a postscript containing this information:

---

47 Maverick, Memoirs, 44.
48 Bollaert, Manuscript, 9.
49 Ibid., III, 11.
50 Kate Mason Rowland, General John Thomas Mason, *Quarterly* XI, 181

Before closing, I am sorry to have to inform you of a sad occurrence...this evening. A man by the name of Fox, while ploughing in a small field immediately on the bank of Shoal Creek, between four and five o'clock was shot down, killed and scalped by Indians! A negro was also in the field at the same time but made good his retreat. The Indians escaped although some pursuit was made. They were supposed to be three in number and armed with rifles...

We may possibly be destined to hear...several events of this character.[51]

This happened in Austin, the capital, and is merely one of the very many instances of disturbances in that western frontier town. An Austin newspaper, in January 1841, carried a story about the murder, at the hands of Indians supposed to be Towaccannies, of James W. Smith, chief justice of the county. Mr. Smith's son disappeared on the day of the outrage, and the newspaper concluded that he had been carried into captivity.[52] Dr. James H. Starr received the following concerning Indian troubles in Austin, from Jack Snively:

The Indians are stalking about through the streets at night with impunity, frequently dressed in white men's Clothing, there is scarcely [sic] a night passes, without some person seeing Indians in Town, they are as thick as hops about the mountains and this vicinity. And occasionally they knock over a poor fellow and take his hair...[53]

---

51 Miller to Sam Houston. MS. Washington D. Miller Papers, (1832-1842) Feb. 23, 1843, No. 4848, Texas State Library, Austin.

52 *Texas Sentinel*, (or *Centinel*), (Austin) Jan. 25, 1840, Aug. 26, 1841, Jan. 31, 1841.

53 Snively to Starr, Aug. 17, 1841, MS. Starr Papers, 1845-1863, File No. 752, University of Texas, Austin.

One of the governmental officials of Austin reported that Indians were such a menace around 1841 that "you were pretty sure to find a Congressman at his boarding house after sundown."[54]

These are but a few of the many outrages committed in the vicinity of Austin, which, because of its extreme westerly situation, was a convenient place to attack. However, it was not only the western towns that suffered. A correspondent of the *Telegraph and Texas Register* wrote from Nacogdoches, situated in the extreme eastern section of the country, but far enough to the north to be classed as the frontier, that there was much Indian trouble:

> Mr. Editor, Dear Sir:—The Indians are yet ravaging our frontier. They have stolen, during the last month, thirteen horses from this neighborhood, and on the 26th instant, opened our stables, and took four horses belonging to my brother, together with bridles etc. Mayor Waters, myself, and two others started early next morning in pursuit...[55]

And a few months later, the same paper carried an article on a similar occurrence in Goliad, a town situated in the southwestern section of the country, and a great distance from Nacogdoches. Horses again were the object of the raid. Leaving Goliad with their new mounts, the Indians went to the nearby town of Copano, where they overtook seven wagons loaded with merchandise.[56]

Most of the raids enumerated here were small affairs and did not involve a great number of men. There were however, many general uprisings in which large tribes, often numbering hundreds, were involved. Such was the raid at Linnville, on Lavaca Bay, when about three hundred

54 Lubbock, *Six Decades in Texas*, 143.
55 *Telegraph and Texas Register*, April 25, 1838.
56 Ibid., July 7, 1838.

Warriors attacked the town, carried off a few prisoners and large quantities of food, and destroyed or burned what they could not take along.[57] General uprisings of this kind are too well known to be recounted here.

This is only half of the story, for the Texans were not standing by idly while Indians lurked in the neighborhood. Looking through the same set of sources again, we find other Indian stories—this time with the names reversed. The *Texas Sentinel*, that carried the story of the murder of Chief Justice James Smith, carried this article at about the same time:

> A party of five Indians…were killed in Weber's Prairie twelve miles below this city, [Austin] on Monday last. A large party of citizens are in pursuit of another party, discovered in that neighborhood.[58]

And Mrs. Maverick who told of the Indian methods in her Memoirs, likewise recounts the methods the white man used to protect himself:

> Mr. Maverick was a member of the Volunteer Company of "Minute Men," Commanded by the Celebrated Jack Hayes…Each volunteer kept a good horse with necessary equipments and arms, and a supply of coffee, salt, sugar & other provisions ready to start on fifteen minutes warning, in pursuit of marauding Indians. The signal was given by the Cathedral bell, and the men generally responded promptly to the call.[59]

The *Telegraph and Texas Register*, that gave many an account of uprisings, also mentioned that at times bands of

---

57 Maverick, Memoirs, 42.
58 *Texas Sentinel*, Jan. 28, 1841.
59 Maverick, Memoirs, 22.

twenty or more volunteers patrolled the countryside and kept a constant watch for surprise attacks.

When the Red Men became particularly bold and invaded the Brazos region, to within about seventy miles of Houston, the government intervened and ordered a battalion into the field under the command of Major Bonnell.[60] This band of men did noble work, and while there were many alarms of reprisals, the people in the vicinity were well protected and there was no killing or stealing during the three months these men patrolled the territory.[61]

Men who lived in the frontier regions protected themselves by being well armed at all times. Here is the way Mr. Sparks arranged to protect himself and his family, and to carry on his regular work at the same time:

> I hired a young man by the name of B. F. Sells to live with me, as much to help protect my family as to work for me. We would take our guns with us to the field to plough, and we would leave one gun at one end of the rows and one at the other; then we ploughed so that he would be at one end and I at the other, so they [Indians] could not cut us off from both our guns.[62]

Some citizens of Texas, even those living in the troubled sections, were evidently not much concerned about the ever-present menace. Thus James Nicholson wrote to his wife that even the women and children had no fear of the Indians, and frightened them away.[63]

With this idea of Nicholson we might well conclude the discussion on Indians. The Red Man was an everlasting

---

60 Lubbock, *Six Decades in Texas*, 84.
61 Ibid., 89.
62 Recollections of S. F. Sparks, *Quarterly*, XII, 75.
63 James to Mrs. Nicholson, June 27, 1838, Nicholson Papers.

annoyance and danger, but really was no match for the white — at no time during the history of the Republic was the superiority of the white man ever threatened, and while progress in overcoming the Indian was slow, it was steady; the growing Republic gradually, sometimes with the loss of life, pushed the Indian beyond the advancing frontier.

The Dumb Belle & The Jockey: Amusements

The life of the average Texan was a hard one, a constant, grim struggle for existence, made more or less severe depending on the individual. Yet it was a life that had its compensations. To the ordinary joy and happiness that came as a reward of accomplishment, was added a constant round of amusements. These pioneering people were ever-ready for entertainment, and a gathering of almost any sort was usually a signal for merriment.

The most formal kind of all the amusements probably was the theater. Already in the spring of 1837 an effort was made by G. L. Lyons to bring a company of dramatists to Texas. Mr. Lyons had had wide experience in the theaters of the United States, and was at that time playing in the Saint Charles Theater, New Orleans.[1] Nothing however came of the proposal, and the project was dropped.

The following year, 1838, when the idea was revived, the citizens of Houston became enthusiastic and eagerly looked forward to the introduction of the drama. On May 26, the *Telegraph and Texas Register* announced that John Carlos had already built a theater and that a company from the States was on its way to Texas.[2] On June 11, 1838, the new theater was formally opened with a presentation of "Sheridan Knowles's celebrated comedy, The Hunchback." The second play of the evening was the farce, "The Dumb Belle." The whole company sang a new Texan anthem, composed especially for the occasion by Henry Corri, the director of the company.[3] The Houston *Telegraph* gave this account of the play:

> The Theatre in this city was opened on Monday Evening last. The house was crowded to

1 *Telegraph and Texas Register*, April 4, 1837.

2 Ibid., May 26, 1837.

3 Ibid., June 16, 1838.

overflowing, and many citizens were com-
pelled to wait on the outside, being unable to
obtain seats. The opening address was deliv-
ered by Mr. Carlos in a very appropriate manner and was received with general applause.
It was pleasing to notice the remarkable for-
bearing disposition shown by the audience for
these pioneers of the drama. Indeed, we believe that if the playing had been of the most
ordinary character, it would have been com-
mended on this occasion by our citizens, with
the most cordial good nature; fortunately,
however, indulgence has not in the least degree been required, as the actors have ex-
ceeded the expectation of their most sanguine
friends. It must be exceedingly gratifying to
every true friend of the drama, to behold its
infancy in our country attended by such favorable auspices.4

The following week the *Telegraph* reported that the theater was still well-attended and that the performances were
excellent. "The Stranger," "Therese," "The Rent Day,"
"Maid of Munster" and "The Robber's Wife," were some of
the plays given, and they "were performed in a style that
would have gained applause even upon the stages of the
principal cities of the United States."5

The *Telegraph* of August 11, 1838, announced that in a
few days the Theater would be closed for the summer, to
reopen in October under the auspices of Henry Corri.6 And
in the fall when the theater was to reopen, the same paper
carried the announcement: "Mr. Corri has recently been
making exertions to render the Houston theatre worthy of
public patronage...We have been pleased to notice in the

4 Ibid., June 16, 1838.
5 Ibid., June 23, 1838.
6 Ibid., Aug. 11. 1838.

selection of his pieces, he has an eye to those having a tendency to mend the morals of his patrons."[7]

In January, 1839, the steamboat, Rufus Putman, docked at Houston, bringing John Carlos and a theatrical company that had been engaged in New York.[8] The company was to open on January 21, 1839 with the "fashionable comedy, Charles the Second or the Merry Monarch," and the second play of the evening was to be "The Secret, or Hole in the Wall."[9]

The *Telegraph* for March 13, 1839 announced that Henry J. Finn, "the celebrated comedian" was in the city and would appear at the Carlos theater for several evenings. Mr. Finn was billed in this fashion: "This accomplished Actor and Scholar, who has been for many years the favorite of the American Boards, has been engaged for a few nights...In all his walks of life, Mr. Finn is recognized as the well-bred gentleman, and the most original actor now living in either country."[10]

This was the day of the traveling stock company, and it is not surprising to see that many different sets of players in making the rounds stopped at Houston, for in 1839 it was the principal center of the theater-goers in Texas. Companies followed each other in rapid succession; two weeks after Mr. Finn made his appearance the arrival of Charles H. Eaton was announced — "justly distinguished tragedian" who had made his debut at the Tremont in Boston as Richard III.[11]

A perusal of the various advertisements for the spring of 1839 gives some idea of the plays that were enacted. On April 17, 1839, "The Irish Ambassador" was announced.[12] Three days later it was "Romeo and Juliet" with Emma Barker

---

7 Ibid., Nov. 10, 1S38.

8 Ibid., Jan. 2, 1839.

9 Ibid., Jan. 19, 1839.

10 Ibid., March 13, 1839.

11 Ibid., March 30, 1839,

12 *Morning Star*, April 17, 1839.

playing Juliet,[13] and the following week it was "Timour the Tartar."[14] On May 4, the "Cateract of the Ganges" and "The Lady of Lyons"[15] were announced. It was quite common to give two distinct plays each evening, in fact that was the usual procedure; "Conanchio," an Indian drama, and "Mazeppa,"[16] in which sixty Houston men played, were billed together. "Mateo Falcone, or the Brigand Boy,"[17] was presented alone on May 7. But the following week there was a double bill again, this time "The Green Eyed Monster" and the farce "Catching an Heiress."[18]

Toward the end of 1840, the Telegraph gave news about theatrical performances at Galveston,[19] but from this time on there are fewer notices about the drama. Evidently Galveston started to give Houston some competition; at least later announcements seem to indicate as much—Mr. and Miss Wyman and Company were scheduled to appear in Houston after having fulfilled an engagement in Galveston.[20]

Before taking leave of the professional dramatist, it might be well to illustrate how the newspapers wrote up the leading characters. On August 13, 1845 the "Lady of the Lake" was given at Houston; the dramatic critic, in reporting the story, commented on the large crowd that attended in spite of the heat, and then wrote about Mrs. Hart:

> This lady…has become justly popular among the admirers of the drama in this city…She looked well — played well and with great effect. She is gifted with strong feelings and a nice discrimination — she has the power to draw a tear, or win a smile — and sings well.

---

13 Ibid., April 20, 1839.

14 Ibid., April 29, 1839.

15 Ibid., May 4, 1839.

16 Ibid., May 6, 1839.

17 Ibid., May 7, 1839.

18 Ibid., May 13, 1839.

19 *Telegraph and Texas Register*, Oct. 18, 1840.

20 Ibid., June 19, 1844.

She is what some of our boys would call a charming little actress.[21]

Besides these professionals there were many amateur dramatists in the various towns. James N. Smith, who taught school in the log house in Gonzales county in 1840, tells how an amateur theatrical organization sometimes came into being:

> My school consisted of a mixed school for young men and young ladies and boys and girls, and there were several young men and ladies living in the upper & lower settlement as it was then called, the young people would assemble at Mrs. Blairs of a Saturday evening to sing and learn vocal music...After a while Doctor Duck proposed to my son James and the two young Scotchmen that they would endeavor to establish a theatre for acting of plays. He composed some very good pieces, and those who took part would prepare themselves, and the singings sometimes give way to the Theatre. Those young men...could perform very well and they introduced the others, so that once in two weeks they met at Mrs. Blairs to act...[22]

The town of Matagorda had not only an amateur company, known as the "Thespian Company of Matagorda," but even had a distinct little theater building.[23]

In addition to this group entertainment, single entertainers would often tour the countryside and stop at the various towns. The *Northern Standard* of Sept. 17, 1842 announced that "the well known and unrivalled" ventriloquist, E. L. Harvey was in Clarksville. Tickets to the performance were

21 Ibid., Aug. 21, 1845.
22 Autobiography of James N. Smith, 25-26.
23 Bollaert, Manuscript, I, 128.

fifty cents each.[24] Harvey reached Nacogdoches by December, and on the seventh of that month, Adolphus Sterne wrote in his diary: "a ventriloquist named Harvey amused the people this evening with his rare powers."[25]

Men like Mr. Harvey who toured the country, came in contact with a great many people and offered their powers of amusement to large and small communities alike. The same cannot be said about the theater; it had a decidedly limited appeal; only city folk, and usually only those in the larger cities, could benefit from this form of entertainment. The residents of small towns and the country folk had to look elsewhere for amusements, and usually found them in patriotic celebrations, and in public and private gatherings of one kind or another.

The anniversary of Texas Independence was always a day of general rejoicing, gala celebrations and festivities of all kinds. It was celebrated "by the Sunday and other schools, by the military companies, literary institutions, religious societies & the citizens generally..."[26] "The more humble citizens" at times patronized this day with what was known as a "Dutch Ball." The Bollaert manuscript gives an interesting description of this form of entertainment:

> One dollar is the price of admittance, I paid my fee and entered. The room was small and badly lighted; the music—such as serves our other Balls. The attendance—slim; only ten or twelve Ladies and some twenty Lords. Altogether it was rather a failure in this instance. But then—this was the commencement of the season. A large ball room, music, lights, ladies—will increase & multiply, as the season advances.

------

24 *Northern Standard*, Sept. 17, 1842.

25 Sterne, Diary, *Quarterly* XXXIV, 347.

26 Bollaert, Manuscript, II, 218.

I only aspire to a general description, and cannot entertain you with an account of how the belle was ornamented, and the beau equipped. In fact these balls are intended more for use than for ornament; for dancing than gazing. Republican simplicity is the order of the day. The women, make themselves as tidy as circumstances allow; holding a correspondence in colors, and an adherence to any particular fashion, in utter contempt. The men, I am sorry to say, carry this contempt for dress a little too far—with some exceptions.

Country dances, cotillions and waltzes, followed each other in rapid succession. Partners were rather 'scarce & in demand' but I managed to 'hold my own' among the competitors. 'In Rome etc' is my motto, and from being a dignified spectator, I soon be came a jolly and eager participant. Some of the ladies made their debut 'on the light fantastic toe',… they were encouraged and prompted…and did very well.[27]

The fourth of July was another day of general rejoicing. References to the celebration of this day are most numerous. The citizens of Danville got together at a huge barbecue with many speeches and patriotic addresses.[28] Houston celebrated it in such a way that the editor of the paper seemed to think it was unpatriotic: "All seemed to forget that it was the national holiday of a foreign country; all nationality was for the season completely lost, our citizens forgot that they were Texans and, transported with an unpatriotic ardor, celebrated as Americans the national festival of the parent

---

27 Ibid., I, 39.
28 Estill, Huntsville, *Quarterly* III, 267.

republic."[29] Preparations to celebrate this day in a fitting way at Galveston in 1838 were pretentious. A special committee held preliminary meetings. Through its efforts an excursion from Houston to Galveston was organized, the steamer Sam Houston was pressed into service, and all arrangements were made so that Galveston could be host to the Houston citizens and celebrate this day in one grand get-together.[30]

The anniversary of the battle of San Jacinto was likewise usually the signal for festivities. In 1837 the city of Houston held a never-to-be-forgotten ball to commemorate this event. By boat and on horseback the revelers came from Brazoria, Columbia, San Felipe, Harrisburg and the surrounding country. When Sam Houston, the hero of that famous battle, entered the ballroom to be greeted with "Hail to the Chief" from the orchestra, the ball got under way, and, interrupted only for dinner at midnight, it lasted until dawn.[31]

Sometimes people simply got together, had a barbecue, and finished the occasion with a dance which lasted until morning. More often an election furnished the occasion for the barbecue and ball. Mrs. Dilue Harris tells in her reminiscences of the barbecue and ball she attended on September 1, 1836, at Stafford's Point. "The barbecue, ball and election were at Mr. Dyer's near our house. The people came from different settlements and several of our Harrisburg friends were there…There was no drinking or fighting. The ladies spent the day quilting. The young people began dancing at three o'clock and kept it up until the next morning…Mother had ripped up an old silk dress and made me a ball dress…That was my last ball at an election. After that there was too much whiskey drunk for ladies to be present."[32]

But evidently the ladies did not stay away entirely from these affairs. Adolphus Sterne attended his first one in 1843

---

29 *Telegraph and Texas Register*, July 7. 1841.

30 Allen to A. Ewing et al, June 28, 1838. Ewing Papers, 1835-1838, Texas State Library, Austin.

31 Lubbock, *Six Decades in Texas*, 57-60 cites *Ladies Messenger*.

32 Reminiscences of Mrs. Harris, *Quarterly*, IV, 183-184.

and wrote in his diary: "…about 800 persons were assembled, they done ample Justice to the Barbecue, and to my surprise (not having seen it afore) some 600 Ladies were present and partook of the Barbecue, and after the Repast, the Candidates for the Senate made Speaches as a matter of course they promised much—the Candidates for the lower House also Spoke."[33]

Gatherings of all kinds were common: The Masonic Fraternity celebrated;[34] Zavala county found enough pretext, at a visit of the President, to give an all-night dance and barbecue;[35] and the citizens of Columbia commemorated the victory of Conception with a ball in honor of the participators.[36] The correspondence of Mirabeau B. Lamar and Ashbel Smith is filled with invitations to public dinners, balls, suppers and parties. "The pleasure of your company is solicited to a Dinner to be given in Honor of General Henderson at the Tremont House, this evening at 3 o'clock, January 13th, 1840,"[37] or again, "Col. and Mrs. Love request the pleasure of Dr. Smith's company on Tuesday evening."[38] These are typical of the many invitations found.

Another common form of amusement was horse racing. The track at Velasco, near Houston, was one of the famous ones during the Republic; there were many others in various parts of the country. Races were well-patronized and the horses usually compared favorably with the better steeds of the famous race horses in various parts of the world.[39]

Even New Orleans was favorably impressed with the caliber of racing in Texas, and the *Weekly Picayune* carried this story in 1838:

------

33 Sterne. Diary, *Quarterly*, XXXVI, 215.
34 *Telegraph and Texas Register*, June 26, 1839.
35 Looscan, Elizabeth Huling, *Quarterly*, XI, 67.
36 *Telegraph and Texas Register*, Oct. 11, 1836.
37 Printed invitation; Ashbel Smith Papers.
38 Written invitation; Ashbel Smith Papers.
39 Smith to Barnard, Dec. 20, 1838, MS. Ashbel Smith Papers.

The citizens of our neighboring Republic pay considerable attention to the improvement of their blooded stock. Fine horses are raised, and the sports of the turf are to be enjoyed in their full vigor. The races over the New Market Course, at Velasco,...are to come off in the first week of May. The Club comprises some of the most eminent names of the country — among whom, we see that of Dr. Archer as President; the Hon. W. H. Wharton, Gen. Felix Huston and Gen. T. J. Rusk, as Vice President; and Col. Wm. Ryon, as Secretary and Treasurer. The purses to be run for all liberal in their dimensions; the arrangements for the accommodation of visitors will be of the most ample nature that the newness of the country will afford; and, from the level face of the country we presume that the track will be highly favorable to the sport. The town is situated immediately on the sea-coast, at the mouth of the Brazos de Dios, and it is at all times a place of great resort from all parts of the Republic. It is only from two to three days run from this city — so that we may expect to see crowds going down upon the Columbia and other vessels, to enjoy the pleasure of the trip, together with the excitement and interest of attending the New Market Races in Texas.[40]

The Texas papers carried many announcements about the Velasco and other races: "splendid and refined amusement" was promised to those who would attend.[41] Branch T. Archer, president of the club, invited Dr. Smith to attend the spring races at Velasco by saying: "We shall have one week

---

40 *The Weekly Picayune* (New Orleans) April 16, 1838, Typewritten copy; University of Texas, Austin.

41 *Telegraph and Texas Register*, March 31, 1838.

of raceing [sic] and frolic in this town (commencing on the twenties of next month)...I will insure you a display of fashion & beauty..."[42] If this did not bring Smith, then maybe General Thomas Green's additional "Many fine women & horses are in attendance all ready"[43] did.

The various entries in Sterne's diary seem to indicate that the races were well-attended. On August 28, 1843, Sterne wrote: "All hands are gone to Douglass where a big Horse race is going to take place,"[44] and some time later Sterne again wrote: "Several San Augustin folks gone through to Douglass where a Race is to be run tomor-row."[45] Even the poorer people and farmers attended these races, and, not having much money, they gambled their stock.[46] In addition to public celebrations, races and the like, there were literally dozens of other forms of entertainment ranging from large house parties down to small groups of boisterous merrymakers in the taverns and saloons. Candypulling contests were usually enjoyed by the younger set. Some forty or fifty "lads and lasses" would congregate and the sport would take place in the afternoon. The frolic would be followed by music and dancing in the evening. It was easy to arrange a party of this character.[47]

A quilting party required much more preparation. It was simply a variation of the "log rolling" idea, the frontier method neighbors had of helping each other do the kind of work that required many hands; this particular variety usually meant a party. Mr. Cox, in his reminiscences of early Texas, gives a very good account of one of these quilting parties. According to Mr. Cox, the people came early and worked industriously because the quilt had to be finished before the real fun began. When all had arrived the quilt was

---

42 Archer to Smith, Feb. 19, 18.19, MS. Ashbel Smith Papers.

43 Green to Smith, Feb. 17, 1839, MS. Ashbel Smith Papers.

44 Sterne, Diary, *Quarterly* XXXVI, 217.

45 Ibid., XXXVI, 222-223.

46 Wallis, *Sixty Years on the Brazos*, 48.

47 Bollaert, Manuscript, II, 173.

was stretched, men and women took their places, and the work began. The men took their position on the ground and they were "expected to roll up the sides as fast as needed, to pass the thread & scissors—and with anecdotes and small talk to entertain the workers." While this was going on the kitchen was also a scene of much activity. There the "biggest turkey" on the place was "basking his back before a huge log fire," and a little porker was being groomed in the "bottom of the oven." And there were "Pies, Cakes, Chickens, Eggs, Butter, Milk, Preserves..." all being given final attention, so that the supper given to the workers after they had finished the quilt, might in some measure recompense them. But the third part was still to be enacted. It commenced "ere the fragments of the feast" were all cleared away. The fiddler took his place and called out the numbers, dancing commenced, and continued until coffee and cake were served at daylight, when, "with reluctant partings, the company scattered."[48]

Then the "Fancy Fairs," usually conducted for some charitable end, were always signals for get-togethers, and independent of the charitable ends for which they were conducted, they were "distinguished apologies" for mirth.[49]

Also, weddings were solemnized with all-night feastings. The friends of the participators in this drama would arrive long ahead of time; and after "the bridegroom with the bride under his arm, supported by the necessary attendants" were brought before the minister, and the "I wills" were pronounced, formality would be dispensed with and festivities would go on through the night.[50] A christening would be conducted in much the same fashion. After the minister performed the ceremony, the well-wishers would carry out their part of the program.[51]

Music was not entirely neglected, and it afforded many an evening's entertainment. Occasionally a concert was given

---

48 Reminiscences of C. C. Cox, *Quarterly* VI, 127.
49 Bollaert, Manuscript, I, 108.
50 Ibid., II, 163.

but this was quite an unusual event; there are not many references to formal concerts to be found. Bollaert records one given by Mr. Seefeld at the Tremont House in Galveston. He attended but did not have much to say in its favor as the "Piano was screwed up to a G" and the concert poorly rendered.[52]

The principal musical diversions were of a private nature. Several people would assemble and entertain themselves. Mrs. Holley in writing to her sister refers to a gathering of this kind: "Mr. Hammerkin had his piano brought into the parlor below & last evening we had a little concert, of the household, around it. He & I performed, with the vocal aid of Mr. Allen…"[53] Sterne notes a similar event in his diary: "The Misses Sims came down and we had Music on the Piano till 10 P. M."[54] Pianos were rare during the Republic; those who had them probably brought them along when they came to the country. At times a merchant got possession of one and then advertised the fact. S. Browning, an Austin dealer, had "an elegant mahogany 6 octavo Piano forte; by Cragg, quite new," for sale.[55]

Particular localities had their own forms of amusements. Thus San Antonio, almost exclusively Mexican throughout the greater time of the Republic, had its fandangoes and other kinds of Spanish amusements. William Bollaert, who spent some time in this city, took an evening off, and in company with some of his San Antonio friends, watched the "Maromeros," or provincial rope dancers and actors perform. He put this little account of the event in his notes:

> The company consisted of a comical Payaso or clown, three young men and one female. The performance was *al fresco* in the court yard of a house in the public square. At the foot of the

---

52 Ibid., I, 76.

53 Holley to Brand, Nov. 12, 1842., MS. Holley Letters.

54 Sterne, Diary, *Quarterly*, XXXIV, 73.

55 *Texas Sentinel*, May 13, 1841.

the tight rope was made two large fires, this being the only illumination for actors and audience. The rope dancing over, tumbling commenced, this being finished, upon a rude stage, a comedy and two farces followed, the three pieces occupying about twenty minutes. I cannot speak favorably of the polish composition of the dramas represented.[56]

Even the Slaves had their own amusements. Plantation owners gave them a week off at Christmas time, and then "be decked & in their best, they visit each other, the evenings ending in singing and dancing."[57] Bollaert, who took many notes on the amusements of the Texans, will be drawn on again for an illustration of negro amusements. To quote him directly:

> Last night [Dec. 31] through the kindness of Mr. Mc —— the Negroes of this vicinity had their Christmas Ball in his unfinished store... It was late ere all arrived, many of them having had to come several miles. It was a 'Subscription Ball' & the unfortunate Negro who could not raise a couple of bits was not admitted at the commencement of the Ball, but Black hearts wax soft & as midnight approached & the Strains of Music sweet, the excitement produced by dancing, the door Keeper became benevolent & it was a public ball...
>
> About midnight they had supper & to it they went until daylight when they returned to their respective homes, their Christmas holidays having terminated.[58]

---

56 Bollaert, Manuscript, II, 107.

57 Ibid., II, 370.

58 Ibid., II, 181.

Lastly, but by no means the least of all the places of general amusements, there was the saloon. Some writers try to give the impression that every second door in a town led into a saloon; while this is an exaggeration, it nonetheless creates a correct impression because there were many saloons. It will not be necessary to discuss the possibilities of merriment and jollification from resorts of this kind. Nor will it be necessary to demonstrate that any ordinary get-together was greatly enlivened by the introduction of spirits. Suffice it to say that conditions in Texas in this regard were much the same as elsewhere.

That early Texans had such variety of amusements and distractions was quite fortunate, but not at all surprising. The same wide range was found in every phase of their existence.

As we have seen in these pages, the men who founded the Republic were not daunted by the problems of its development. They attacked the problem of daily existence, supplying the body with food, clothing and shelter. They provided for the soul, offering it the consolations of religion, and for the mind, proposing for it the benefits of education. For the health of the body politic, they set up courts of justice and grappled with difficulties of finance and transportation. Finally, when work was done, or not for the moment pressing, they learned to relax in pleasant recreation.

Bibliography

Printed Material
Manuscripts

Addison, Oscar M. — Papers, April 18, 1834 – Dec. 31, 1850. University of Texas, Austin

Bollaert, William E. — Papers, Personal narrative of a residence and travels in the Republic of Texas during the years 1840–1844. Newberry Library, Chicago.

Erskine, Michael — Diary and Letters, Blucher Hays Erskine, editor. University of Texas.

Ewing, Alexander — Papers, 1835–1838. Texas State Library, Austin.

Hartzo, Daniel — Diary, Feb. 1, 1841 – Dec. 31,1846. University of Texas, Austin.

Herndon, J. H. — Diary of a Trip from Kentucky to Texas. University of Texas, Austin.

Holley, Mary Austin — Correspondence, 1808-1846, Photostatic copy. University of Texas, Austin.

Hunt, Memican — Papers, 1838–1848. Texas State Library, Austin.

Johnson, Moses — Correspondence 1834–1852. Photostatic copy. University of Texas, Austin.

Maverick, Mary A.—Diary, 1842–1845. Possession of Mrs. Norval J. Welsh, San Antonio.

Maverick, Mary A.—Memoirs, 1881. Possession of Mrs. Norval J. Welsh, San Antonio.

Maverick, Samuel — Papers, 1838–1859. University of Texas, Austin.

Miller, Washington D.—Papers, 1832–1842. Texas State Library, Austin.

Nicholson, and William—Papers, 1838–1839. University of Texas, Austin.

Smith, Ashbel—Papers, 1823–1886. University of Texas, Texas.

Smith, James Norman—Autobiography. University of Texas, Austin.

Smyth, George W.—Papers, 1832–1865. Texas State Library, Austin.

Starr, James H.—Papers, 1845–1864. University of Texas, Austin.

Van Zandt, Isaac—Letters, 1835–1847. University of Texas, Austin.

Printed Matter

Braman, D. E. — *Braman's Information About Texas*. Lippincott & Co., Philadelphia, 1857.

Gulick, Charles Adams — *The Papers of Mirabeau Bounaparte Lamar*, Edited from the original papers in the Texas State Library. Vols. I, II, III, IV, edited by Mr. Gulick. Vols. V, and VI, edited by Harriet Smither. Vols. I and II published by A. C. Baldwin & Sons, Austin, Texas. Vols. III, IV, V, and VI, published by the Press of Von Boeckman-Jones Co., Austin, Texas.

Houstoun, Mathilda C. — *Texas and the Gulf of Mexico; or Yachting in the New World*. G. B. Zielier & Co., Philadelphia, 1845.

Ikin, Arthur — *Texas*. Sherwood, Gilbert and Piper, London, 1841.

Kennedy, William — *Texas: the Rise Progress and Prospects of the Republic of Texas*. 2 Vols. London, 1841.

Lubbock, Francis R. — *Six Decades in Texas, or Memoirs of Francis Richard Lubbock*. Edited by C. W. Raines, Ben C. Jones and Co., Austin, Texas, 1900.

McCalla, Rev. William — *Adventures in Texas, Chiefly in the Spring and Summer of 1840; with a Discussion of Comparative Character, Political, Religious and Moral*. Printed for the Author, Philadelphia 1841.

Maillard, N. Doran — *History of the Republic of Texas from the Discovery of the Country to the Present Time*, London, 1842.

Moore, Francis — *Map and Description of Texas*. H. Tanner, Jr., Philadelphia, 1840.

Newspapers

Morning Star — *Morning Star* (Houston) April 8, 1839-Oct. 8, 1839.

Northern Standard — *Northern Standard* (Clarksville) Aug. 20, 1842-Dec. 23, 1843.

Telegraph and Texas Register — *Telegraph and Texas Register* (Columbia) Aug. 9, 1836-April 11, 1837. (Houston) May 2, 1837-1845.

Texas Sentinel or Texas Centinel — *Texas Sentinel* (Austin) Jan. 25, 1840-Aug. 26, 1841.

The Weekly Picayune — *The Weekly Picayune*. (New Orleans) Typewritten copy of article in issue of April 16, 1838, University of Texas, Austin, Texas.

Magazine Articles

Adams, Ephraim Douglas — "British Correspondence Concerning Texas." Ephraim Douglass Adams (ed) in *The Southwestern Historical Quarterly*, Vol. XV.

Bryan-Hayes Correspondence — "The Bryan-Hayes Correspondence", in *The Southwestern Historical Quarterly*, Vol. XXV.

Clopper Correspondence — "The Clopper Correspondence 1834–1838", in *The Quarterly of the Texas State Historical Association*. Vol. XIII.

Erath, Lucy A. — "Memoirs of Major George Bernard Erath" in *The Southwestern Historical Quarterly*. Vol. XXVI.

Harris, Lewis B. — "Journal of Lewis Birdsail Harris 1836-1842", in *The Southwestern Historical Quarterly*. Vol. XXV.

Sterne, Adolphus — "The Diary of Adolphus Sterne, Harriet Smithers (ed)" in *The Southwestern Historical Quarterly*. Vols. XXX to XXXVI.

Secondary Material

Books

Brown, John Henry — *History of Texas*. (2 Vols.) Becktold and Co., St. Louis, 1893

Eby, Frederick — *The Development of Education in Texas*. Macmillan, New York, 1925.

Fitzmorris, Sister Mary Angela — *Four Decades of Catholicism in Texas, 1820–1860*. The Catholic University of America, Washington, D. C. 1926.

Gray, William F. — *From Virginia to Texas, 1835, Details of a journey to Texas and return*. Gray Dillage and Co. Houston, Texas, 1900.

Newton, Louis W. and Gambrell, Herbert P. — *A Social and Political History of Texas*. Southwest Press, Dallas, Texas, 1932.

Parisot, Father P. F. and Smith, Father C. J. — *History of the Catholic Church in the Diocese of San Antonio*. Carrico and Bowen, San Antonio, Texas, 1897.

Smithwick, Noah — *The Evolution of a State or Recollections of Old Texas Days*, Nanna Smithwick Donaldson (ed), Gammel Book Co., Austin, Texas. 1900.

Thrall, Rev. Homer S. — *A Brief History of Methodism in Texas*, Nashville, Tennessee, 1889.

Wallis, Jannie Lockhart, in association with Laurance L. Hill — *Sixty Years on the Brazos. The Life and Letters of Dr. John Washington Lockhart 1824–1900*. Privately printed by the Press of Dunn Brothers, Los Angeles, California, 1930.

Magazine Articles

Arthur, Dora Fowler — "Jottings from the Old Journal of Littleton Fowler", in *Quarterly of the Texas State Historical Association*. Vol. II.

Cox, C. C. — "Reminiscences of C. C. Cox", in *The Quarterly of the Texas State Historical Association*, Vol. VI.

Curlee, Abigail — "The History of a Texas Slave Plantation, 1831–1863", in *Southwestern Historical Quarterly*. Vol. XXVI.

Estill, Harry F. — "The Old Town of Huntsville" in *The Quarterly of the Texas State Historical Association*. Vol. III.

Harris, Mrs. Dilue — "Reminiscences of Mrs. Dilue Harris" in *The Quarterly of the Texas State Historical Association*. Vol. IV.

Holland, J. K. — "Reminiscences of Austin and Old Washington", in *The Quarterly of the Texas State Historical Association*. Vol. I.

Kenney, M. M. — "Recollections of Early Schools" in *The Quarterly of the Texas State Historical Association*. Vol. I.

Kleberg, Rosa — "Some of My Early Experiences in Texas" in *The Quarterly of the Texas State Historical Association*. Vols. I & II.

Looscan, Adele B. — "Elizabeth Bullock Huling, a Texas Pioneer", in *The Quarterly of the Texas State Historical Association*. Vol. XI.

Looscan, Adele B. — "Harris County, 1822–1845" in *Southwestern Historical Quarterly*. Vols. XVIII, XIX, and XXII.

Miller, Robert Finney — "Early Presbyterians in Texas as Seen by Rev. James Western Miller, D. D." in *Southwestern Historical Quarterly*. Vol. XIX.

Raines, C. W. — "Enduring Laws of the Republic", in *The Quarterly of the Texas State Historical Association*. Vol. II.

Red, William S. — "Allen's Reminiscences of Texas, 1838–1842" in *Southwestern Historical Quarterly*. Vols. XVII and XVIII.

Rowland, Kate Mason — "General John Thomas Mason", in *The Quarterly of the Texas State Historical Association*. Vol. XI.

Schmidt, C. F. — "Viktor Friederich Bracht, A Texas Pioneer", in *Southwestern Historical Quarterly*. Vol. XXXV.

Sparks, S. F. — "Recollections of S. F. Sparks" in *The Quarterly of the Texas State Historical Association*, Vol. XII.

Strickland, Rex Wallace — "History of Fannin County, Texas 1836–1843", in *Southwestern Historical Quarterly*. Vol. XXXIII.

Winkler, Ernest W. — "The Seat of Government of Texas" in *The Quarterly of the Texas State Historical Association*. Vol. X.

Winston, James E. — "Notes on Commercial Relations Between New Orleans and Texas Ports 1838–1839" in *Southwestern Historical Quarterly*. Vol. XXXIV.

www.ingramcontent.com/pod-product-compliance
Lightning Source LLC
Chambersburg PA
CBHW020455100426
42813CB00031B/3377/J